PENNSYLVANIA DEPART...
195 — SCHOOL YE...

D0733271

ONCE UPON
THE TIBER

Series Editor
JOHN TRAUPMAN

By the same author

DUCES ROMANORUM*
Profiles of Roman Courage

LECTIONES DE HISTORIA ROMANA*

ONCE UPON THE TIBER*
An Offbeat History of Rome

LABORS OF AENEAS*
What a Pain it was to Found the Roman Race

VERGIL FOR BEGINNERS*
A Dual Approach to Early Vergil Study

CICERO THE PATRIOT*

* A teacher's manual is available for these titles

ONCE UPON THE TIBER

*An Offbeat History
of Rome*

Rose Williams

Bolchazy-Carducci Publishers, Inc.
Mundelein, Illinois USA

Editor
John Traupman

Cover & Text Illustrations
Mark Bennington

Once Upon the Tiber
An Offbeat History of Rome

Rose Williams

© **Rose Williams 2002**
All rights reserved.

First published by Wimbledon Publishing Company 2002

Bolchazy-Carducci Publishers, Inc.
1570 Baskin Road
Mundelein, IL 60060 USA
www.bolchazy.com

Printed in the United States of America
2008
by United Graphics

ISBN 978-0-86516-668-4

Library of Congress Cataloging-in-Publication Data

Williams, Rose, 1937-
 Once upon the Tiber : an offbeat history of Rome / Rose Williams ; illustrations,
Mark Bennington.
  p. cm.
 Originally published: London : Anthem Press, 2002.
 Includes bibliographical references and index.
 ISBN 978-0-86516-668-4 (pbk. : alk. paper)
 1. Rome--History. I. Title.
 DG209.W57 2007
 937--dc22

                                                    2007029640

Dedicated to Professor Robert Reid of Baylor

Who taught us to view history from many angles

CONTENTS

INTRODUCTION

The trouble with reading history is that some earnest scholar has organized it into all the pertinent (and usually dreary) facts. Facts, like good bread, need a little yeast and perhaps a mite of salt to be digestible. History is a diary of humans, and even in the most dismal human life funny things happen. It's not taking note of the funny things that drives us to suicide, homicide and general crabbiness. The Romans made quite a splash in human history, and of course any bunch that hung around for 1,200 years had its ironies, foibles and grins. Here you will find the True Facts about Venus the Bald and Marius the Muddy as the ancient writers recorded them. This book ambles through major Roman events and personalities from the time of Aeneas to the time of Romulus Augustulus, visiting soldiers and ladies and entrepreneurs, picking thistles and picking on people. The lives of major Roman authors are included, for in viewing a culture one should always consider the literati. They are even better than the politicians are at taking themselves seriously and everything else in vain.

CHAPTER I

"Fuimus Troes, fuit Ilium."
Vergil, *Aeneid*, Book II, 325

(Once we were Trojans; once there was a Troy.)

The history of Rome, like the history of many great cities, began
Somewhere Else. In this case the Somewhere Else was Troy, a
great walled city standing on a private beach (which was about to
become all too public) on the northwest coast of Asia Minor. Priam,
king of Troy, having 50 sons and 50 daughters, was feeling a bit
overwhelmed by it all. (As he has only one recorded wife, Hecuba,
she must have been even more overwhelmed.) He left his infant
son Paris in the nearby woods on Mount Ida. Paris was, of course,
rescued by a Wandering Shepherd, as shepherds in ancient legend
spent more time in collecting lost princes than in tending sheep.
Paris fared well on Mount Ida, playing the pipes and charming the
nymphs, until a banquet up on Olympus, the holy mount of the
gods, turned nasty.

Eris, goddess of Discord, who liked fireworks even if it wasn't a
holiday, tossed on the banquet table a golden apple inscribed "for
the most beautiful." It was immediately claimed by Venus, who
had the best right to it; Juno, who as Big Mama thought she had a
right to all goodies; and Minerva, who as goddess of wisdom
should have known better. Jupiter (or Zeus, if one is over Athens
way) was far too well acquainted with the female sex to judge this
contest, so he sent them down to Mount Ida, recommending Paris
as an excellent judge of beauty. Somewhat startled at the sudden
overpopulation of goddesses in his small glade, Paris balanced
the golden apple in his hand as he listened in awe to the details of

the beauty contest. The deities didn't waste time with the bathing suit and talent competitions: they got right down to the bribes. Juno promised him power over Europe and Asia; Minerva, victory against the Greeks; and Venus, with a slight smirk, offered the most beautiful woman in the world. Paris broke all speed records giving Venus the apple.

Neither of them worried for a moment about the fact that the most beautiful woman in the world was already married. She was Helen, the wife of King Menelaus of Sparta, and she had been causing havoc among men since her early childhood. A regular platoon of kings, nobles and upstarts had descended on her supposed father King Tyndareus (actually she was the product of one of those little escapades of the god Jupiter, but this is no time to go into that) demanding her hand in marriage. Before he named Menelaus as the lucky man, old Tyndareus, who was no fool, made all the hopefuls swear to support Helen's husband in the quarrels that were extremely likely to arise concerning her. Every man, modestly expecting to be the winner, happily swore the oath. (A few minutes later most of them were just swearing.) When Helen disappeared during a state visit of the Trojan prince Paris, the Greeks descended on Troy with one thousand ships to win her back. (Later kill-joy Greek historians claimed that no army in its right mind would go to all this trouble for the sake of a faithless woman, and that the war really had more to do with Troy's arrogant habit of demanding toll-fare for ship passage in the Strait of the Dardanelles, but what epic poet could get 12 books out of *that*?) Thus came the over-crowded public beach.

For nine long years the armies fought back and forth across that beach. In the tenth year the greatest heroes, Achilles the Greek and Hector the Trojan, were slain and Ulysses, knowing that epic poets like round numbers and the war needed to end in ten years, suggested the Trojan Horse. One morning the Trojans awoke to a strange sight. As they peeped over Troy's walls, they saw the trampled beach with its usual litter of empty wineskins and apple cores, but no Greeks. There was only a grossly oversized rocking horse with no rockers – just rollers – and a nasty look on its face. Unfortunately this unsightly plaything was stuffed with soldiers and provided with a lying witness to beguile the Trojans into

Gift-bearing Greeks

taking it into the city. Laocoön the priest tried to keep the Trojans from falling for this, crying "Beware of Greeks bearing gifts." He should have said, "Beware of gifts bearing Greeks."

CHAPTER II

"Fuge, nate dea, teque his eripe flammis."
Vergil, *Aeneid*, Book II, 289

(Flee, goddess-born, and snatch yourself from these flames.)

Among the Trojan heroes of war was Aeneas, the son of the Trojan prince Anchises and the goddess Venus. As his house was in the suburbs, he missed out on the excitement as the horse disgorged its payload and the Greeks, augmented by their buddies who had sneaked back from their hiding place behind an island, set fire to Trojan houses and skewered the people as they ran out. (This was rather unsportsmanlike, but effective.) Aeneas donned his trusty armor and killed Greeks until his Mama came, took him by the ear and hauled him off to rescue his family. She planned for her son to found Rome, not wind up as a cinder.

Father Anchises made a few choice remarks about the gods' insensitivity in burning his city while leaving him alive, but changed his tune when a sacred flame played over the head of his small grandson Ascanius. Any fool knew that flames playing over the heads of sleeping children were first-rate Messages From The Gods. Aeneas placed the old man on his shoulder and headed out of Troy. Little Ascanius had to run alongside his Papa, holding his hand and being scolded for not keeping up. Aeneas told his wife Creusa to follow him but when they reached the edge of the city she had disappeared. One feeble excuse for this was that she had sat down to rest. While no one called Creusa an intellectual, surely she had more common sense than this. Venus, no doubt having an eye to marriage alliances, was widely suspected of arranging matters so that Aeneas would be a widower.

Ascanius Keeping Up

With his father and son and a disreputable crowd of refugees, Aeneas sailed to the west. After a few unnerving encounters with bleeding bushes and bird-women Harpies, Aeneas, courtesy of Juno, who still got heartburn over that apple business, found himself in the mother of all storms. The next thing he knew, he was tossed, somewhat the worse for wear, on the coast of Africa and wound up as the all-too-welcome houseguest of Queen Dido of Carthage. Aeneas' helpful Mama Venus had sent her mischievous son Cupid to the banquet Dido gave when Aeneas arrived. Disguised as Ascanius, whom Venus had put to sleep in a hidden valley, Cupid got in a little choice arrow work that sent Dido down for the count. Between Dido demanding marriage, Mercury demanding an instant departure for Italy, and Venus and Cupid showing up in various disguises (in those days anyone you met might turn out to be a god), poor Aeneas sailed away in self-defense.

When he arrived in Italy he consulted the Cumaean Sybil, as his father Anchises was dead by this time but still wanted to have his say, and the Sybil knew the way to Hades. It was not easy to go to Hades as Aeneas was not dead and the place was not interested in the tourist trade, but with a golden bough and a good deal of fool-hardiness Aeneas managed it. In Hades he got a guided tour guaranteed to scare him into holiness; a lot of information on what happened to whom; and a rosy picture of Rome's future.

Back in Italy he discovered, as many explorers before and since have done, that the place was already inhabited and the indigenous population was not necessarily thrilled with newcomers. Some long and nasty battles must have reminded Aeneas and his followers (those who had not drowned, jumped ship, or died of exhaustion) of the Old Days in Troy. At last he married the Princess Lavinia and founded a city named Lavinium. Aeneas was the founder of Rome only in a loose literary sense – he had descendants who did the deed.

CHAPTER III

"Tantae molis erat Romanam condere gentem."
Vergil, *Aeneid*, Book I, 33

(So great a task it was to found the Roman race.)

Aeneas disappeared. No one knew exactly where he went, but Dido, who had taken his departure very badly, had prayed to some rather unpleasant deities that he might die before his day and lie unburied in the sand. However that may have been, his son Ascanius, called Iulus (and less printable things from time to time; after all, if anyone ever had a childhood that was an excellent excuse for juvenile delinquency, it was Ascanius), left Lavinium to found Alba Longa. (Many centuries later Julius Caesar would claim that the Julian family line, of which he was so far the chief ornament, was directly descended from Iulus. This not only gave Caesar a Roman family tree that was older than Rome, but supplied him with a bloodline from Venus to explain some of his activities.)

After several generations, Alba Longa was inherited by King Numitor, who had a weak backbone and an unpleasant brother named Amulius. After scaring his brother out of the kingdom, Amulius arranged an early death for his nephew. Numitor's male issue being no more, Amulius honored Numitor's daughter Rhea Silvia by making her a Vestal Virgin (accent on the last word). He reckoned without the god Mars, however, and before Amulius realized that all, from his point of view, was not well, Rhea Silvia was the mother of twins, Romulus and Remus.

Amulius was a religious man. He knew what happened to people if they killed relatives: they got visits from the Furies. Since these immortal female avengers had snakes for hair and eyes that wept tears of blood, nobody really wanted to encourage them to put in an appearance. He reasoned that if he put the boys in the flooding Tiber in a willow basket, however, and they happened to drown, he could not be blamed. After all, if they were really the sons of a god, as that wily-tongued niece of his claimed, they would not be any the worse for a good bath.

Amulius' Worst Nightmare

Romulus and Remus floated onto a sandbar and were found by a wolf with a Mother Hubbard complex. She was soon relieved of duty by the usual Wandering Shepherd, a man named Faustulus. (What a life the wives of shepherds must have had, never knowing how many babies they would have by nightfall.)

Romulus and Remus grew up among the sheep like the Trojan Paris, but they wasted little time on nymphs at this stage of their lives. (Romulus discovered girls later; Remus, thanks to a too-ready tongue, didn't live long enough to grow amorous.) In their youth, when not herding sheep, they hunted game in the forests. Their favorite game turned out to be bands of robbers. As the Roman precursors to Robin Hood, they robbed these robbers and distributed the spoils among their shepherd friends. (This proves that modern politics goes back to the early history of man.) The robbers, who like all really prosperous criminals, could assume the guise of honest men, caught Romulus and his Merry Men in ambush and hauled them before Numitor, who was living in retirement on a portion of his lands given him by his generous usurper of a brother.

Faustulus, who had always had his suspicions about the disappearance of Rhea Silvia's twins and the she-wolf's sudden increase of family, told his story to Romulus and to Numitor. The result was a nice sneaky plot and a neat little revolution that restored Numitor to the throne.[1] Romulus and Remus then found, as a result of all their labors, that they were living in a kingdom whose absolute ruler was their grandfather. Grateful and kind he might be, but his views on long hair, loud music after midnight and pizza for formal banquets did not agree with theirs. So, in 753 BC they set out in search of their own space.

CHAPTER IV

"Romulus, ut geminae stant vertice cristae . . ."
Vergil, *Aeneid*, Book VI, 779

(Romulus, with the double plume [of Mars] on his head . . .)

Remus' Last Leap

The twins soon decided to go back to their wolf cave and found a city somewhat merrier than their grandfather's for their band of Merry Men. This cave was on the Palatine, or Shepherds Hill, which was an excellent strategic location, being one of an irregular ring of seven hills south of the Tiber. Its desirability was enhanced because the Etruscans, whom nobody wanted to meet on a dark night (or on a bright morning for that matter), lived north of the Tiber, and the river was given to flooding. Near the wolf cave on the Palatine, Romulus and his men cut great square blocks of stone and began to build a wall. Remus laughed at the budding fortification and jumped over it. Romulus killed Remus. After that nobody laughed at Romulus' efforts, especially if he might be in earshot. The city was named Rome after Romulus, and nobody laughed at that, either.

As the city grew, Romulus began to take notice of the facts about women; the most pertinent of these was that, in Rome, there weren't any. He and his groupies combed their hair, trimmed their beards, donned clean togas and set off to court the daughters of the Sabines, who lived some three miles away. Their reception threatened to give them frostbite. Nobody, it seemed, wanted his daughter to marry a muscular young ne'er-do-well with no stock portfolio. The girls, whose opinions were not sought, might have felt differently.

Muscular Young Ne'er Do Well

Back in dear old Rome Romulus hid his anger and planned to achieve his objective, fathers or no fathers. After a suitable interval, he invited the neighboring tribes to watch athletic games. "Come and enjoy an outing," his heralds cried. "Bring your lunches, your families – your daughters." Now the neighbors might have had their doubts about the Romans as sons-in-law, but they had none at all about their prowess in sports. The games were well attended. While the fathers were laying bets and watching the athletes, the Romans suddenly began running off to the Temple of Marriage with the girls. Fathers through the centuries have resented this kind of treatment. They went home for arms and reinforcements.

Meanwhile back on the Palatine, the Romans were attempting to soothe their indignant brides. They seem to have succeeded rather well, perhaps because, as Livy says, they remembered that the girls had lost all family, and the new husbands tried to show the kindness that fathers and brothers ought to show but often don't.

Be that as it may, by the time the Fuming Fathers had collected their arsenal and swept down (or up in this case) to the settlement, the girls had had a change of heart. They ran between their fathers and their new husbands and got terribly in the way of any really telling javelin-throwing or swordplay. While the fathers foamed at the mouth and tried to reason with them, the girls started talking about grandchildren. The Sabines grumbled off

Sabine Father Grumbling Off Home

home, as many newly made fathers-in-law after them have done, and a few years later marveled that such rotten sons-in-law could produce such perfect grandchildren.

To help him govern, Romulus appointed one hundred elders, called senators, who sometimes felt that their help was not properly appreciated. One day, during a ceremony, a thick cloud enveloped Romulus, and when the cloud dispersed his throne chair was empty. The people murmured that the senators standing nearby had done away with King Romulus, but the senators swore he had been carried away by the gods. Henceforth he was worshipped as the god Quirinus and gave the senators much less trouble on high than he had on earth.

CHAPTER V

"Qui iuvenes! Umbrata gerunt civili tempora quercu!"
Vergil, *Aeneid* Book VI, 771

(What men they are! Their brows shaded by honor's crown!)

Romulus' sudden promotion left a power vacuum in Rome. Each senator considered himself a likely prospect for king. With everyone getting only one vote, his own, there was a deadlock, and the senators took turns ruling. The common people objected to this, feeling that one master was bad enough, but a hundred masters gave ample cause for a full-scale revolution. The Romans and their unwilling in-laws the Sabines now being joined in a harmonious unity (which quite often hit a sour note), the Sabines demanded that a Sabine be named king. Taking a good look at the truculent faces of the Sabines and the even more truculent faces of the commoners, the senators named a Sabine of learning and excellent reputation, Numa Pompilius, as king.

The new king decided to give Rome law and religion, both of which had been a bit neglected up to now. Anticipating some grumbling and argument, which in early Rome was likely to be backed up with a dagger or two, Numa promptly announced that he held nightly sessions with the nymph Egeria, the deity of a nearby spring of water, and that all his reforms, particularly the less popular ones, were the product of divine inspiration. Ovid, who had a truly modern desire to drag sex into every possible relationship, declared that Egeria was the wife of Numa. However that may have been, Numa's 40-year reign in Rome was a time of peace, and that may well have taken the intervention of a divine spouse.

Numa Pondering Roman Law

After Numa died, full of years and wisdom, Tullus Hostilius was made king. His name is a good clue; he led the Romans back to business as usual, thinking that, until a ruler came along who had enough loot to build a Roman bath, good workouts could be had on the battlefield. In general, the Romans agreed with him but they didn't mind letting somebody else do the fighting while they sat in the shade and laid bets on the outcome. When the Romans and the Albans came to blows over some tit-for-tat cattle rustling, somebody noticed that each army contained a set of triplets of similar age and strength. The Roman Horatii and the Alban Curiatii soon found themselves in the middle of a meadow being cheered on by Good Old Ourside. In the mêlée that followed the three Curiatii were wounded and two of the Horatii were killed. The third Horatius, who had evidently been smelling the flowers and had missed the main event, felt a strange emptiness on his side of the field. He turned and ran, knowing that the wounded Curiatii would be hard-pressed to keep up, and killed them one by one as they followed.

Everybody in Rome was elated by this victory except Horatia, the sister of the winner, who had been engaged to one of the dead Curiatii. Her brother killed her because she was weeping on Rome's day of victory.

Evidently even the Romans thought it was possible to carry civic pride too far; they charged Horatius with murder before the king, who thought this was a great time for a little delegation of authority. He appointed a pair of judges, called duumvirs. (This noble title comes for the Latin for "two men," and has no negative connotation as to their mentality.) The duumvirs pronounced Horatius guilty, and worthy of death by scourging "either within or without the pomerium." Horace had no taste for a scourging death either inside or outside and, at the prompting of King Tullus, who just loved violent men, he appealed to the people. At his trial his father, who thought a daughter or two lost in the flush of victory a small price to pay, spoke for Horatius, and the people released him on condition that he do suitable penance. Horace passed under a yoke of subjection called "the Sister's Beam" which was erected in the street. This was interpreted both as a sign of humility and a handy instrument for brushing aside the sister's ghost. He was said to hurry inside on dark nights ever after, to escape her vengeful spirit. Hopefully it finally caught him.

CHAPTER VI

"Ancus iactantior, nimium gaudens popularibus auris . . ."
Vergil, *Aeneid*, Book VI, 815

(Ancus the boastful, rejoicing too much in popular favor . . .)

Boastful or not, Ancus Marcius was a successful king, but the world's worst judge of character. Having made an intimate friend of an adventurer from Etruria who had given himself the name of Lucius Tarquinius Priscus, Ancus proceeded to make this man the guardian of his children. After the death of Ancus, Tarquin Priscus sent Ancus' sons on a hunting trip at the time that the people were choosing a new king and then held his own political pep rally. He got the kingship and lost no time in doubling the number of senators, thus setting up his own personal congressional party.

In all his dubious achievements, Tarquin Priscus was aided by the advice of Tanaquil, his formidable soothsayer of a spouse, who could always find a prophecy to fit whatever she wanted. In their palace one evening a slave, wandering around doing his chores (or trying to avoid them) was somewhat upset by finding a servant-child sleeping with his head on fire. The startled minion raised an uproar that brought the whole palace, king and queen included, to investigate. Tanaquil restrained a practical servant who was about to douse the child with water, and commanded that the sleeper not be disturbed. When the child, Servius Tullius, awoke, the flame disappeared and he was unharmed. Whether she knew the story of Aeneas' son Ascanius or had some unexplained scheme of her own (which was usually the case), Tanaquil declared that this was a divine sign that the child should be brought up with the king's own children. This was done, and Tanaquil saw to it that her daughter Tarquinia was married to Servius Tullius. This was not destined to be one of the happiest marriages of all time, and did great damage to the fine old adage "Mother knows best."

Meanwhile the by-passed sons of Ancus Marcius had been biding their time. After biding it for 38 years, which surely was enough to lull suspicion, they sent a pair of shepherds to appeal to the king, which they did by burying an axe in his head. Tanaquil at once had the court cleared of all men but Servius Tullius. Telling the people that the king, who by now was extremely dead, was recovering and wished them to obey Servius Tullius, she placed in Tullius' hands the power, which he lost no time in solidifying. When the captured shepherds squealed on their employers, the sons of Ancus Marcius were exiled. Servius settled into firm control and at last dared to announce that – guess what – the king had expired.

Servius, having no desire to spend the next 38 years watching over his shoulder for the two sons of Tarquin Priscus, married Lucius and Arruns Tarquin to a pair of daughters he happened to have. This by no means satisfied the princes, but an opportune war with Veii and other Etruscan cities unified the people. (The Etruscans never minded fighting a little war, even when it obliged a neighbor.)

Returning home, Servius Tullius established the first Roman census. Any citizen of a modern state could have warned the Romans that a census is likely to lead to both taxation and military service, but the poor souls trod blindly to their doom. Now the king knew how many Romans there were and, worse still, how much property they had. They soon found themselves providing equipment for their newly defined status in the military and fighting some cheery little wars in the seasons when the crops didn't need their attention. Every man between the ages of 16 and 47 served in the field, while the elders guarded the city. This went a long way to prevent juvenile, and even senile, delinquency.

Servius then built a wall around the city, which had begun with the Romans on the Palatine Hill and the Sabines on the Capitoline; Tullus Hostilius had added the Caelian and resided upon it; Ancus

Marcius had assigned the Aventine to newcomers. Servius expanded Rome to include two more of the seven hills – the Quirinal and the Viminal. He increased the small settlement on the Esquiline and went there to live. He believed, poor innocent, that the presence of a king would improve the reputation of the place.

Building On The Seven Hills

CHAPTER VII

"Vis et Tarquinios reges animamque superbam . . . videre?"
Vergil, *Aeneid* Book VI, 817

(Do you also want to see the Tarquin kings and their
haughty spirit?)

Servius Tullius' great misfortune was that he was completely surrounded by Tarquins. Due to his mother-in-law's meddling, his wife was a Tarquin and not one of the better ones. At least one of his two daughters, although she might be named Tullia, had all her mother's nasty sense of superiority. Due to his lamentable attempt at foresight his sons-in-law were also Tarquins. The historians say that one of Servius' two daughters (both called Tullia, after the fine old Roman tradition of keeping the family name intact and letting confusion fall where it may) and Arruns, one of the young Tarquins, were nice young people; unfortunately they were married to the not-so-nice pair and were soon dispatched by their mates, who then married each other. After that it was only a matter of time for old Servius.

Lucius Tarquin summoned the senate without the king's knowledge. When the aged king rushed in, he was flung down the steps and murdered. After hastening to the Senate House to hail her husband king, Tullia drove her chariot over her murdered father's body – a notable instance of a nasty child whom maturity did nothing to improve.

Lucius Tarquin, called Superbus (the Arrogant), now set out with enthusiasm to earn his nickname. He seized authority and killed all the senators who he thought had favored Servius; then, dispensing with such old-fashioned habits as consulting the senate and appointing judges, he killed or exiled many other powerful people whose influence he feared or whose property he desired.

As young Lucius Junius Brutus narrowly observed these grue-some proceedings, he decided his safety lay in stumbling around, saying stupid things and generally behaving as if a few tiles were missing from his mosaic. Biding his time, he waited for the proper moment to indulge in a little republic founding. This came in 509 BC when Sextus Tarquin, a true chip off the old block, raped Lucretia, the wife of Tarquin Collatinus, because she was not only beautiful but moral, and decency was one thing he couldn't stomach.

Lucretia was an early exponent of the stern old Roman doctrine that suicide was preferable to a number of disagreeable existences. Once she had called her father and husband and told them and the rest of Rome what had happened, she killed herself in full view of all the people. Brutus waved the dagger she had used on high and, in a stirring speech, called the Romans to battle against the despi-cable Tarquins. Hardly pausing to wonder how the dull and stupid Brutus had suddenly blossomed into both orator and warrior, the Romans rallied to his cry. They drove the king and his family into exile.

This sudden turn of events left a power vacuum and, as Tarquin hadn't left much of a senate, some provisions for leadership had to be made by the Roman people. After his census, Servius Tullius had divided the people into *comitia centuriata*, which jaw-breaking title came to refer to voting groups, even though Tullius was probably thinking about the military. The *comitia*, which could hardly be blamed for a distaste for one-man rule, elected dual presidents, later called consuls, to serve for one year. They then provided for a lively future by decreeing that these men should serve as supreme commander on alternate days. Lucius Junius Brutus and Tarquin Collatinus were chosen as the first consuls. The people settled down under their new government to put things back together, having promoted *rex* or "king" to the status of dirtiest word in the Latin language.

Rex had only one serious competitor in the dirty-word sweep-stakes; that was "Tarquin." After thinking it over for a while, the Romans decided they didn't want anyone named "Tarquin" running the government, even every other day. They said that although they realized that Tarquin Collatinus was a nice guy, and that he had suffered greatly at the hands of his unspeakable relatives, they would still feel more comfortable if the walls of Rome were between him and them. Tarquin said he understood and withdrew – lock, stock and barrel – to Lavinium before anyone got any funny ideas about confiscation. Publius Valerius, who had no nasty name problem, was chosen consul.

Tarquin Collatinus Ponders His Moves

CHAPTER VIII

"Qui iuvenes! Quantas ostentant, aspice, viris!"
Vergil, *Aeneid* Book VI, 771

(What men they are! What strength they show, behold!)

Of course no one expected the Tarquins to take all this quietly, but they delayed a while, seeking reinforcements, before descending on Rome. Meanwhile some of the privileged young Romans were discovering that life under an impartial law, rather than under a despotic and licentious king, could be restrictive. Among those who missed the grand old orgies at the palace and became embroiled in a plot to restore the monarchy, were the sons of Lucius Junius Brutus, who had been hailed as father of his country but was shortly to be deprived of being the father of anything else. A stool-pigeon slave carried the whole king-restoration plot to Brutus, who set about capturing the traitors and taking an eager headcount to see if anyone in the line-up bore a family resemblance to himself. He found his two sons in captive lot, and then had the unenviable duty of ordering all the traitors to be stripped, scourged and beheaded. He did his duty with a wooden countenance, then went almost with relief into the war the Tarquins finally mounted and died there.

Defeated in this attack, the Tarquins went whining to Lars Porsenna, king of Clusium and general overlord of Etruscans. Porsenna was not averse to teaching these republic-loving upstarts a lesson and installing a friendly king in Rome. He collected a massive army, thinking that 90,000 seemed a nice round number, especially since the total population of Rome, including women, children and puppy dogs, was somewhat less than that. As the

Etruscans tramped southward, stirring up immense clouds of dust and making Italy a perfect Hades for asthmatics, they forgot Romulus' foresight: Rome had been built on the south side of the Tiber, partially because they lived on the north side. Furthermore the river, feeling frisky at the moment, was flooding like crazy.

There was one bridge across the Tiber. When the Romans saw that crowd of dusty Etruscans, they sneezed and beat it across said bridge. One stalwart soul, however, Horatius Cocles (this means One-eyed; he'd been to war before), took up his position on the narrow bridge and refused to budge, ordering the Romans to cut the bridge down behind him while he held the far end against all comers. Two shame-faced Romans came back to help him, and the Etruscans halted at the river's edge and had a good laugh. They threw a great many spears, all of which some skilful shield-work deflected. Before they could decide just who should charge those wicked-looking little Roman swords, the bridge timbers cracked. Larcius and Herminius, Horatius' companions, darted back across the falling bridge. Horatius, having gotten in a few choice last words about the failings of the Etruscans, jumped into the Tiber and was carried across to Rome by the flood.

Rivers, however frisky, settle down after a while, and Porsenna laid siege to Rome. This charming tactic of ancient warfare consisted of surrounding an enemy city, seeing that no one entered or left and laying bets on how many days it would be before the inmates ate the last rat and starved to death. A young Roman named Gaius Mucius, who was a finicky eater and didn't like rats, asked the senate for permission to sneak over to the Etruscan camp and kill the king. Whatever they thought of the chances of success for this ambitious project, the senate gave consent. After all, they didn't like rat either.

Mucius solved the disguise problem by throttling the first Etruscan sentry he could sneak up on, donning his armor, and strolling calmly into the camp. Here he met a problem; he had no Etruscans coins in his tunic and therefore hadn't the foggiest idea what the king looked like. He didn't like to ask; an Etruscan soldier should know such things. Besides, his Etruscan had a definite Latin accent. He decided to use logic: seeing a huge silk tent in the middle of camp and a richly dressed individual in front of it

Mucius Solves the Disguise Problem

paying the soldiers, he leaped upon the dais in front of the tent and killed the payer. This story will serve as a good explanation of why professors of logic are so seldom great warriors: an even more richly dressed man stepped out of the tent and demanded, "Why have you killed my secretary?"

Mucius did not think this was the moment for lengthy explanations; he had already created an uproar, especially among the soldiers who had not yet been paid. He leaped from the dais and hacked wildly with his sword in every direction. A number of soldiers lost all interest in their paychecks, and indeed everything else, but Mucius was at last overcome and dragged before the king.

"Who are you?" demanded the king, who by this time was understandably a good deal annoyed. "My name is Gaius Mucius," was the reply. "I am a Roman citizen." This last remark was unnecessary; Porsenna had probably figured that out for himself by now. "I wanted to kill my enemy," said Mucius, still giving in to his penchant for stating the obvious. "I know how to die; a Roman can both give and endure pain. But know this: 300 young Romans have sworn that they will neither eat nor drink till you are dead. The man who brings your food tomorrow may be your slave, or he may be a Roman."

Porsenna was a high-spirited warrior and a powerful king, and he did not take kindly to being threatened by his own prisoners in his own camp. "Bring a burning brazier," he howled, "and fry this upstart until he tells us everything!" Mucius thrust his right hand into the fire and watched it burn. "This," he said, "is what a Roman thinks of pain."

Porsenna decided that if Horatius Cocles and Mucius were fair samples of what Rome had to offer, it might be time that he got back to urgent business in Clusium. He set Mucius free, not really knowing what else to do with him. He offered peace to the Romans and went back to his own kingdom, leaving his Tarquin cousins, whom he suddenly realized he had never really liked anyway, to their fate.

The Romans welcomed the hero Mucius with great joy and some tangible rewards, one of which was a field across the Tiber that became known as the Mucian meadow. Mucius also got a new nickname, Scaevola, which means "Lefty," because he had lost his right hand. One wonders why he didn't have the good sense to put his left hand in the fire. Considering the quick thinking he showed, however, in coming up with that tale about the 300 conspirators, he may have been left-handed all along.

Luckily for Rome the Etruscans were totally unable to keep their noses out of foreign wars that might bring them a few advantages. They had teamed up with the Carthaginians, who were trying to muscle in on Greek Sicily while the Persians were belaboring the Greek peninsula. The Persians and the Carthaginians were defeated in this grandiose scheme, and Etruria found out about the high cost of losing.

Meanwhile the Latins who lived south of Rome decided they liked kings better than the Roman senate and began saying so with swords and spears. At the Battle of Lake Regillus the Romans defeated these upstarts with the help of the gods Castor and Pollux, who not only fought for the Romans but thoughtfully put in an immediate appearance in the Roman Forum and announced the victory. For this double duty as warriors and war correspondents they were rewarded with a magnificent temple in the Forum, parts of which are still visible today. As for the Etruscans, they agreed to a treaty of peace to last for the usual 40 years. In ancient Italy, however, a 40-year peace treaty was usually rudely curtailed.

CHAPTER IX

"Roma, felix prole virum."
Vergil, *Aeneid* Book VI, 784

(Rome, fortunate in the men she breeds.)

Italy is basically a long mountain chain with a beach on each side. Rome, thanks to Romulus' selection of the seven hills just south of the Tiber River, lay a few miles from the river's western shore, about halfway down the length of the peninsula. In the beginning she was only one of numerous small settlements dignified by the name of cities. The Romans were energetic little devils though and were generally victorious in the inevitable fights with the neighbors.

They also had good luck against the mountain people. These last didn't grow much food, as their perpendicular homes weren't conducive to farming; they preferred to steal what they needed from their neighbors. The Romans came to be the usual leaders in following the mountaineers home and whamming the daylights out of them to reclaim the grain, cattle, women and other miscellaneous booty they had carried off. It gradually dawned on the Romans, however, that like washing dishes, this reclamation job was barely finished before it had to be started all over again. Perhaps, if one got a peace treaty out of them while they were still licking their wounds, and maybe left an overlord in charge up there, some of this regular exercise could be prevented. Colonies of Roman settlers in strategic spots wouldn't be a bad idea, either. And on the strength of the warlike reputation Rome had been earning, maybe a few treaties of alliance could be arranged with groups they hadn't even had to lick yet. So through conquest, colonization and alliances, Rome slowly spread her power north and south along the peninsula.

Since Rome was content with control of high policy and allowed the cities under her power to run their own local affairs, and squabble about them as much as they pleased short of war and mayhem, things went fairly smoothly. Roman taxes, while irksome, were usually not unbearable. The Romans, farmers to the core, opined, "You can shear a sheep every year; you can only skin him once." Since other great powers were much more addicted to the skinning process, Rome's allies usually stuck with her in murky situations.

Meanwhile, back home things were far from rosy. After the kings had been dispatched, the senators and their relatives were known as patricians, a name taken from *pater* or father, signifying that they were ancestors of the state. Everybody else was a plebeian. The patricians claimed to be descended from the gods, and on that score to be the only ones suitable to give sacrifices, as the gods only recognized their own relatives. (Gods were rather short-sighted in those days.) Since all officials had to be priests as well as politicians, these godly descendants had no problem holding on to the chief elective spots in the new *res publica*.

The plebeians had to man the armies, pay the taxes and in general do all the hard stuff while the patricians had all the power. Social climbing was sadly shackled, also, as plebeians couldn't marry patrician girls. If a patrician girl ran off with a handsome plebeian and married "beneath her," the children were illegitimate. Plebeians had a terrible self-esteem problem and, lacking psychologists to blame everything on their childhood and philosophers to tell them that all this humiliation was good for the soul, they decided to take action.

Poor people always have one advantage over the rich: there are more of them. Some bright plebeians realized that this advantage counts for most in war. When the next skirmish flared up, the plebeians withdrew to a mountain a few miles away and left the Roman patricians to fend for themselves. It didn't take an Athenian scholar to see what was likely to happen next. After the patricians cursed and pulled their hair awhile, they sent their wiliest-tongued politician to talk the plebeians back to town.

This politico, Menenius Agrippa by name, told a story about a

Sacrificing To Relatives

human body whose parts got mad at the stomach because they all
worked to feed the stomach, which did nothing but gobble.
Agrippa said that the hand, the mouth, the teeth and the throat all
made a pact to do nothing to feed the stomach, and as a result
starved themselves. He said that the senate was like a stomach
which took in resources and relayed the benefits to all. The plebeians, not being trained in spotting weak analogies, were
impressed and agreed to come back to town, but on condition that
they be allowed to elect plebeian tribunes to protect the interests of

the common man in government. They might not have been oratory majors, but those plebeians knew how to extract some benefits
from a favorable situation.

A little later the marriage restriction was removed and plebeians
were even allowed to run for the elective offices, at least theoreti-
cally. However, the patricians still had the ear of their "relatives,"
the gods. The will of the gods was determined by signs and omens,
such as the flight of birds and flashes of lightning, and the patricians were very good at observing and interpreting these, whether
they were there or not.

CHAPTER X

"Spes unica . . . populi Romani Lucius Quinctius."
Livy, *Ab Urbe Condita*, 3, 26

(Sole hope of the Roman people, Lucius Quinctius.)

Many distinguished Romans of the early days were small farmers, and we do mean small. (Perhaps, if a man had to do all plowing and sowing either by his own strength or with the help of a reluctant mule, extensive acres didn't sound so good.) Lucius Quinctius Cincinnatus was busily tending his four *jugera* (slightly less than three acres of land) when he was called upon to get his fatherland out of a governmental (and monumental) foul-up. The two consuls for the year 458 BC had set out to deal with both the Sabines and the Aequi, two of Rome's usual assortment of enemies. Nautius was supposed to destroy Sabine fields and Minucius was supposed to take on the Aequi armies. Once encamped in enemy territory, however, Minucius lost whatever nerve he may have had and would not leave his camp. The enemy, quick to note this interesting fact, threw up earthworks around the camp and besieged it. Five horsemen, who evidently had more backbone than their commander, managed to break through and take the news to Rome.

The Romans had always suspected that the day might come when having two consuls, especially if they disagreed, could stymie things. They had provided, therefore, that in times of great emergency a special commander-in-chief, called a dictator, could be appointed to hold supreme power for a period of six months. They felt that Cincinnatus was the man for the job, but he was right in the middle of spring plowing.

The messengers of the state arrived in the field where Cincinnatus was working madly. After politely saying hello and making a few remarks about the weather, they requested Cincinnatus to put on his toga. (This long, snow-white, cumbersome wrap-around was only donned by a Roman citizen when he needed his dignity and wasn't about to do anything athletic, such as mounting a horse.) "Oh-oh," thought Cincinnatus, "this doesn't sound like good news." After he had a quick cleanup and was properly be-togaed, they hailed him as Dictator. Then they hauled him off to a boat to cross the river to the city, where he rounded up soldiers, gave orders, made demands and in general acted dictatorish. Then he marched his recruits off to save Minucius, who was still sitting in his camp like a sardine in a can.

Not even pausing for breakfast after a night march, Cincinnatus' troops sounded the battle-trumpet and attacked the surrounders of Minucius. Suddenly the Aequi found themselves the meat in a very nasty sandwich. Minucius' soldiers, hearing a Latin shout coming from outside the siege-works, raised a cry and charged forth. When the swords stopped clanging and the survivors were counted, Cincinnatus had a victory. He took the enemy camp, where his soldiers were delighted to find the makings of a really good breakfast.

After a quick triumphal parade and a few celebrations, Cincinnatus resigned the dictatorship and hurried back to his plowing. He had spent quite enough of the peak planting season on outside distractions.

Meanwhile the plebeians were having trouble with the powerful again. At least in the Bad Old Days of the kings a plebeian accused of anything from murder to bad debt could appeal to the king. The founders of the republic assured the people that they could appeal to the magistrates but the magistrates changed every year, and folks thought they would feel better if all the rules were written down in some nice, permanent, public form – like a few tablets of stone in the middle of the Forum. So in 452 BC ten men, sensibly called decemvirs, were appointed to write what turned out to be the Law of the Twelve Tables.

CHAPTER XI

"Camillus, parens patriae conditorque alter urbis."
Livy, *Ab Urbe Condita*, 5, 49

(Camillus, father of his country and second founder of the city.)

Time, and Rome, moved along. The Romans moved up the scale from fighting with (and defeating) their neighboring tribes and took on the Etruscans on their own territory. After a ten-year siege of the great Etruscan city of Veii had produced little result, the Roman dictator Marcus Furius Camillus discovered that the people of Veii believed that their city could never be conquered while there was water in Lake Albanus. Never one to balk at a little engineering challenge, Camillus had the lake drained and took the city.

Next he besieged the Etruscan city Falerii, where a schoolteacher with an unpleasant scheme for adding to his retirement plan sneaked his young charges, who just happened to the sons of the city leaders, out of the city to the camp of Camillus. There he demanded gold for handing over these children whose parents would surely surrender the city to get them back. Camillus might be big on drainage projects but he balked at using children as weapons, and sent them back to their amazed parents, who surrendered the city. After all, why sit around snacking on withered vegetables and rats when a man of such quixotic notions was your enemy? He might even have some pleasant ideas about generous surrender terms.

The Romans were very pleased with Camillus for his unusual ways of winning battles, as they spared both materials and men, but he soon fell out of favor. There was grumbling because he drove white horses, symbolic of the gods, in his triumphal parade. There was much louder grumbling because somebody suspected he had divided the loot unequally. Camillus found himself on the outside of Rome looking in.

The Romans couldn't have chosen a worse time to throw out a hero. Around 390 BC tribes of Gauls began to move down from northern Italy into Etruria and to wage war on the Romans. These barbarians were truly worthy of the name, being big, untamed and unwashed. In battle they had little discipline, but men of their size fighting like circle saws didn't seem to need it. At the river Allia they not only defeated the Romans but sent them flying back into the city without even closing the gates. The Romans didn't stop running until they reached the citadel, a fortification on the Capitoline Hill. Here they were besieged by the Gauls and things got so tough that Roman women gave their hair for bowstrings. (Later, when the trouble was over, this sacrifice was commemorated by a dedication to Venus Calva – that is, Venus the Bald.[2] As Rome remained standing rather than turning into a smoldering ruin, Venus evidently accepted this in the spirit in which it was meant and chose not to turn mifty about it. After all, for many years she had been accepting tributes in the temple of Venus Cloacina – Venus of the Sewer.[3] Sometimes a deity has to take gratitude where she finds it.)

Camillus got the Romans out of this dismal situation by raising an army of neighbors and rushing to the rescue. He then got his turn at being second founder of the city, which the Gauls had left in a somewhat disheveled state. The achievements of Camillus got bigger and bigger as years passed, and his novel notion of winning wars by honorable behavior made a lasting impression on later generations.

The Romans, in meandering up and down the Italian peninsula, found themselves regarded with suspicion by Tarentum, a large and somewhat feckless Greek city on the southern coast of Italy. The Tarentines seemed to live by the motto "If it looks like fun, do it." In a fit of boisterous excitement they destroyed a small Roman fleet sailing peacefully into their harbor, never seeming to realize that the Romans were likely to resent this. They crowned this folly by insulting Lucius Postumius, the Roman representative sent to discuss the issue. They laughed hysterically at a drunk who befouled Postumius' snow-white toga, until the Roman promised to wash it in Tarentine blood. They had a sneaking suspicion that this was not standard laundry technique, and stopped to ponder his meaning.

Tarentine Considering Roman Laundry Technique

Realizing at last that they had been monumentally stupid, the Tarentines panicked and called in King Pyrrhus of Epirus, one of an endless stream of Greek leaders who thought they could imitate Alexander the Great. To the Tarentines' dismay and disgust they found that he expected them to fight, not just pay his soldiers. He expected other things they didn't like, too – complete control, for example. The Tarentines knew that the Romans by contrast were always willing to let even conquered peoples manage their own personal squabbles; Rome had enough of those to deal with at home. Pyrrhus, however, had to have a finger in every pie and he didn't make very many friends.

Meanwhile he was getting his own nasty shocks. When he first saw the orderly precision of the battle array of the Roman "barbarians" (everybody was a barbarian to a Greek – sometimes even other Greeks) he said "Oops! In war these barbarians are not barbarians at all." He won his battle with the Romans, largely because he cheated by springing a bunch of war elephants on the unsuspecting fellows, who had never seen an elephant before. These animals look a little weird to a neophyte at best, and they are not much more attractive with little gazebos on their heads, each containing a spear-thrower with a wicked aim.

Pyrrhus walked over the battlefield after he had won, looking at all those dead Romans with wounds in front; elephants or no, nobody had run. He also looked over the fine soldiers he had lost, and chalked it up as what would forever be known as a Pyrrhic victory; that is, one which goes in the record books but isn't worth the cost.

He was soon to learn that the live Romans were quite as disconcertingly resolute as the dead ones had been. Having arranged a meeting to discuss returning Roman prisoners, he ran headlong into Fabricius, whose attitude fitted right in with that of the Romans who had died out on the battlefield. First he scorned Pyrrhus' gold and then he refused even to jump when Pyrrhus arranged for a concealed elephant to trumpet behind him. Pyrrhus had a sinking feeling that Fabricius was telling the truth when he said that he was impressed neither by bribes nor by threats. The king returned the prisoners gratis, as there really didn't seem to be much profit to be made from them.

He sent Cineas, his golden-tongued orator, to a Rome he thought ought to be properly humbled by now so that he could arrange a peace. The senate listened to him, but while it was debating the matter, Appius Claudius Caecus, old and blind, had himself carried into the Senate House and proceeded to give a speech in which he said that if the senators did not see that Rome could and must fight off Pyrrhus, they were blinder than he was. The senate sent Cineas back to Pyrrhus with a flea in his ear and a high opinion of Roman determination.

As if Fabricius and Appius Claudius weren't enough, Pyrrhus had to contend with Dentatus as well. Early in his career of making Rome's enemies wish they had picked on somebody else, this prime example of a Stern Old Roman Commander had put the Samnites in their place in 290 BC. Later he had been approached by them one evening while he was in his tiny hut cutting turnips into a pot for his evening meal. When they had offered him a large amount of gold to change sides, or at least throw the contest, he had told them what they could do with their gold and stated his preference for his turnips. Confronted by a talented soldier so totally blind to his best interests, what could they do but lose the contest? If only Pyrrhus had paid more attention to the chapter on Samnites in his Recent History Reports, he might have been better prepared for the defeat Dentatus handed him in 275 BC.

Old Fabricius, in the midst of the heated war with Pyrrhus, had remembered to take a leaf out of Camillus' diary. When he had received a note from Pyrrhus' doctor offering to poison the king for money, Fabricius had sent the note to the king with some sage advice about choosing friends and enemies. He seemed to think that Pyrrhus was pretty poor at both. This may have been true, or perhaps Pyrrhus was just unlucky. After making life merry for opposing armies in Italy and in Sicily for years, in 272 BC he went home for a parade and was finished off by a rooftile thrown by a woman who evidently was not one of his admirers.

Pyrrhus had been the first extra-peninsular enemy the Romans had faced. He and his elephants had contributed quite a bit to Roman education but, as the Romans extended their power to the southern tip of Italy, they were about to tangle with a set of much tougher teachers. The island of Sicily, only 18 miles from Italy, was in the hands of the Carthaginians. The Romans called these residents of Africa the Punic people because they had been refugees from Phoenicia, but they were soon to learn there was nothing puny about them.

The Carthaginians were not impressed with the Romans. They had visited Rome on one of those fact-finding diplomatic missions, and, while being entertained at the homes of the highest officials and senators, had observed that night after night they were eating from the same set of best dinnerware. They soon figured out that the Romans had only one, which was passed around from house to house for Distinguished Company. Being a nation of traders and money collectors themselves, they did not in the least understand that among Romans thrift was a badge of honor and rich men were suspect. It would take centuries for normal human greed to take hold of the Roman psyche. The Romans saw no need for maintaining a great lot of dust-catchers on which they would need to waste many good labor hours of polishing. The Carthaginians were outraged at this barbaric contempt for luxury, which not only showed that the Romans were hopeless hicks but also, if it spread, would definitely be bad for business. They roared with laughter about the Romans, but they laughed a little too soon. They were soon to learn that the Romans kept a fine supply of swords. Being a great sea-faring people, the Carthaginians boasted that no one washed his hands in the Mediterranean sea without their leave. The Romans, always interested in bathing, took umbrage at this.

CHAPTER XII

"Vetus Carthaginem opulentia praefert."
Ausonius, *Opuscula*, Book XI, 2

(Ancient wealth exalted Carthage.)

Both Rome and Carthage wanted Sicily and the time-honored solution to such an impasse is to duke it out. But Carthage fought with a navy; Rome, with an infantry. War under these conditions can be trying, if not impossible. The Carthaginians were fool enough to lose a warship near the shore of Italy, so the Romans hauled it in, looked it over and copied it. Having no sailors, they filled their new ships with soldiers.

Now most people know that naval battles are won by running two ships together; whoever doesn't sink wins. Nobody told the Romans the rules. They put a pulley device with a gangplank in each ship, then rowed up beside the Carthaginian ship, lowered the gangplank, marched across and killed the Carthaginians. Maybe it was unorthodox, but it worked.

The Carthaginian homeland of Africa was invaded and at Rome's mercy until the senate withdrew the main army and left a small force under Regulus in command. Regulus was a hard fighter and an honorable man. In battle he was like a war horse; in peace negotiations he resembled another equine species. When the Carthaginians offered peace he made impossible demands, such as a huge money payment, the islands of Sicily, Sardinia and Corsica, and the surrender of the entire Carthaginian fleet. Infuriated, the Carthaginians put Xanthippus the Spartan in charge of their forces.

Xanthippus, a mercenary soldier native to a land and a city not known for passivity, promptly reorganized the Punic army. He then defeated and captured Regulus, who had been so confident that he had not even secured a line of retreat. Sent home on condition that he would be free if he got Rome to make peace, Regulus insisted that Rome would win if she continued the war. His advice, which turned out to be good, was taken. Regulus returned to Carthage to be killed by the most unpleasant method Carthage could devise, which was sure to be pretty horrific. Pig-headed he may have been, but no one ever said Regulus wasn't brave.

During the next few years, while the Romans were trading insults with the Gauls who lived in northern Italy, Hamilcar of Carthage, who had become commander in Sicily near the end of that First Punic War fracas, was plotting revenge on the Romans. He took his son-in-law and his three sons to Punic territories in Spain and built a power base there. The eldest of those sons, a precocious boy named Hannibal, in later years would have made Papa proud.

Since anybody with a brain would expect the sea-faring Carthaginians to attack by sea, in the summer of 218 BC Hannibal decided to march overland from Spain through the Pyrenees, then the Alps and down into Italy. He seems to have thought that the Alps were just more hills, like the Atlas Mountains in North Africa. He soon learned his mistake. His army fared poorly in the Alps, but his war elephants fared even worse on those narrow cliff paths. Later generations of Romans found the natives of the valleys of the Alps hostile to all foreigners, perhaps because they remembered those elephants crashing through the roof.

Everyone agreed that Hannibal was a military man of great genius. Juvenal says that when the Alps opposed him, he split the mountains with vinegar.[4] Now Juvenal was not only a poet but a satiric poet, and everybody knows they are allowed to lie a lot and to use Figurative Language. Hopefully the above is an example of that language. Surely a busy man like Hannibal, with his mind set on pulverizing Romans, would have had little time for weird geological experiments.

Hannibal defeated and slaughtered one Roman army after another, but he encountered two aspects of the Romans that were so different from regular humanity that they ultimately defeated him. The first was the astounding fact that one could defeat the Romans, slaughter their men and utterly rout them, but nobody could make them realize that they were finished. Pyrrhus could have told him about this disconcerting trait: if you killed every Roman soldier once and some of them twice, Rome would raise another army from some source – allies, freed slaves, or Jupiter only knew what else – and come at you again.

The second odd aspect of the Roman psyche was the "shear 'em – don't skin 'em" philosophy. Hannibal was confidently expecting that as his victories mounted the Italian allies of Rome would join him. However, after taking a good look at their life under Rome, which wasn't too bad, and the nasty habit the Carthaginians had of crucifying anyone who annoyed them, most of the allies stuck with Rome.

After Rome had endured a series of shattering military defeats at Hannibal's hands, old Quintius Fabius Maximus decided that the best way to deal with Hannibal was by not fighting him until Scipio Africanus could grow up. Hannibal was far from home, and the Carthaginians tended to forget that their armies liked their little luxuries, like food, unbroken weapons and whole uniforms. Ravaging the fields of Italy provided only poor sustenance for Hannibal's army, and Fabius saw to it that Carthage never got to win a battle, because he was never where Hannibal thought he would be at fighting time. This behavior earned Fabius the title of Cunctator, or Delayer, and made the high-spirited young Romans (the ones who weren't already dead, that is) think rather poorly of his courage, but it saved Rome.

After 16 years of making life a perfect Hades for the Romans, Hannibal was called home because Publius Cornelius Scipio, soon to be nicknamed Africanus, had finally grown up and taken charge of things.

From his youth this son of a whole line of Scipios had been a thorn in the Carthaginians' fleshy parts. Before he was 17 he had saved his father (also Publius Cornelius Scipio – the Romans must have saved a mint on monogrammed luggage) at one of Hannibal's little get-togethers, the Battle of Ticinus. He had rallied the Roman troops (what was left of them) after their less-than-successful encounter with Hannibal at Cannae. He had gone to Spain as

Son of a Whole Line of Scipios

commander and, treading faithfully in the footsteps of Camillus and Fabricius, had impressed the Spaniards equally with his skill at war and his chivalry when confronted with helpless captives.

One story in particular showed him in a light that would delight any romance novelist, but which had its root in history and economics. One evening his soldiers (who had strict orders to bring to their commander any odd objects they stumbled over, such as spears, nuggets of gold or stray girls) brought a young woman into camp. Scipio not only questioned her (no doubt in a combination of sign language and bad Iberian) but also looked her over carefully in a strictly practical way. He noted that her dress, if somewhat bedraggled, was of good cloth with embroidery around the hem, and that her hands, which would have been the better for a good washing, were uncalloused. These not being the attributes of a nobody, Scipio sent out a fact-finding mission to discover who was missing a valuable girl. Word came back that he had hit the jackpot – she was the daughter of a distinguished family and the fiancée of Alucceius, the young chief of the Celtiberi. When the above-named dignitaries of the opposition were summoned to the Lost and Found Department of Scipio's camp, they brought a wagonload of gold for a ransom; these so-called barbarians were under no illusions as to what had brought the Greeks, the Phoenicians, the Carthaginians, the Romans and anyone else who could sail a leaky craft to the shores of Spain.

Scipio with a flourish restored the girl (unharmed, though still somewhat dirty) to her thankful family. He refused the gold, saying that he only wanted the Spaniards to be friends of the

Romans and, if they felt he was a good man, to know that there were many Romans like him. (This last statement may simply have reflected Scipio's patriotic pride or he may have thought he was correct – the Spaniards were to learn, however, that it fell lamentably short of the truth.) When the grateful parents departed with the girl and refused to take the gold with them, Scipio gave it to the prospective bridegroom as a dowry. A few days later Alucceius showed up with a large cavalry contingent and a desire to join the Roman army. So, for making his soldiers turn in anything they found, returning the girl in good order and forgoing a wagon-load of gold, Scipio had spared Roman manpower and material some battles and gained an extra cavalry for his army.[5] Any accountant would consider this an excellent financial report, not to mention the major public relations coup.

Had Hannibal had enough leisure to consider the matter and had he not been cursed with tunnel vision on the matter of winning wars by killing everybody, he might have realized that here was a formidable enemy indeed. No slouch on the battlefield, Scipio was also a creative thinker and he had not wasted his time in history class. Time was running out for Carthaginian power.

Now Scipio showed the good sense to invade Africa and the Carthaginians at last felt compelled to get Hannibal back home – and fast. It didn't do any good, though; near Zama in North Africa Scipio defeated Hannibal in 202 BC and became BMOR – Big Man of Rome. Old Fabius the Delayer was given the ancient *corona obsidionalis* that a Roman army had always presented to a general who single-handedly saved it from desperate peril. This signal honor, which boasted only about ten recipients in all of Roman history, was a plain grass wreath. The early Romans were never inclined to be spendthrifts.

CHAPTER XIII

"Virum mihi, Camena, insece versutum."
Livius Andronicus, *Odissa*, I,1

(Tell me, Muse, of the cunning hero.)

No one could deny that the century from 300 BC to 200 BC had been one of military unpleasantness, which had left the populace rather inattentive to the finer things in life. During this period, however, something totally unexpected had sneaked up on Rome – the Birth of Literature. Back at the turn of the century Appius Claudius Caecus (possibly before he became Caecus, since the word means blind) had written some speeches, but such things are expected of senators. People were more impressed with his Appian Aqueduct, which brought water to Rome, and his Appian Way, which brought supplies and tourists. Literature, that which can be used in school to make students' lives difficult through endless memory lines and interpretations, ambled up from the south with Livius Andronicus, a Greek slave from Tarentum who was brought to Rome in 272 BC. He became a schoolteacher and needed something for the kids to memorize. Having looked over the extant material, such as the racy Fescennine verses, he hastily translated the *Odyssey* into Latin. He also produced some plays and a lyric poem, which Livy thought was pretty unpolished but which was well received, possibly because 27 lovely maidens danced through the streets chanting it. His *Odyssey* remained the cross for schoolboys to bear for centuries.

The next poet on the scene was Naevius, who saw no point in going to Greece for heroes. He wrote historical plays, an epic and

Andronicus' Lyric Was Successful

comic plays, all about good, and not so good, old Romans. Unfortunately some of his wittier remarks upset the Roman aristocrats, who could never take a joke on themselves, and he found himself in the hoosegow. After his release he again came out with one too many clever sayings and fell afoul of the powerful Metelli clan; thus he wound up his life in Utica in Africa.

Plautus, who saw all too clearly what Naevius kept letting himself in for, confined his comic characters to Greece and saw to it that any Romans represented were properly disguised. As a result, he had great success, a good time and a peaceful death.

Quintus Ennius in his epic stuck to the greatness of the Catos and the Scipios, not their failings, and achieved both some memorable literature and a serene old age.

Roman writers were often more properly Romans Who Happened to Write, as they were likely to be politicians who had an axe to grind or a policy to defend. Such was Cato the Censor, who was born between Punic Wars One and Two and spent a long life living up to his title with zest and gusto, even before he was elected to it. One threadbare toga and a crust of bread were enough for him and he didn't see what anybody wanted with more. As a military commander he was tough, fair and thrifty; as a governor he traveled on foot with one slave; as a farmer he worked beside his slaves and ate what they ate.

His fellow Romans, encountering more and more of Greek *la dolce vita*, just weren't in tune with this Stern Old Roman attitude. Who did Cato think he was? OK, so he admired Dentatus and had a farm near the old warrior's simple hut; was that any reason for going to extremes?

As if his general attitude wasn't bad enough, Cato fell foul of the women. Back in 215 BC, while Hannibal was rampaging up and down the Italian peninsula, flattening fields and wreaking havoc, and the Romans were down to their last few spearpoints, one of the emergency money-raising measures passed had been the Oppian Law, which forbade women to own more than half an ounce of gold, to wear multi-colored dresses or to ride in two-horsed vehicles in Rome. Twenty years later Hannibal had been not only defeated but also driven out of Carthage, and the ladies seemed to think the emergency was over. Cato was consul when they took to the streets in a suffragette-type demonstration demanding the repeal of what seemed to Cato a reasonable and desirable statute. He gave a fiery speech against this blatant proof of female foolishness. The trouble with the Roman senate, however, was that after the consul spoke somebody else got a chance. As usual there was a Liberal spokesman handy and so well did he make the case for allowing Roman women the same privileges that provincial women enjoyed that he won the vote. Some of the senators may have been influenced by the thought of their wives breathing fire out in the Forum.[6]

Later on, the honest men elected Cato censor in truth as he already was in spirit. He lowered the fat content of the Roman Upper Crust. When he wasn't laying taxes on luxuries, fining senators for extravagance, cutting pipes that secretly stole water from the public supply, or scaring tax collectors into remitting their receipts to the treasury, he found time to write quite a few books. He said he despised both Greek and poetry, and the only way he could see for his son to get a decent education was to write the texts himself. Between his histories, speeches and agriculture manuals, the poor boy must have had a mound of homework.

Ladies Expressing Themselves in the Forum

After the Second Punic War, Accius and Pacuvius wrote some tragedies, Terence wrote some comedies, and everybody who was anybody put literature aside until it was time for the Golden Age.

CHAPTER XIV

"Huic maxime malo fuisse nimiam opinionem ingenii."
Nepos, *Alcibiades*, 7

(What hurt him most was his great opinion of his own worth.)

Until the Second Punic War the Romans and Greeks had not really banged heads and discovered how little they had in common, outside of an overweening desire to put their neighbors in their place. Although Southern Italy and Sicily had many Greek cities and King Pyrrhus of Epirus had come over and stirred things up in Italy for a time, close association with all its perils was yet to come. After the defeat of Hannibal, which broke Carthaginian power, King Philip V of Macedon – who was all too prone to confuse his abilities with those of his predecessor Alexander the Great – set out to add the city-states of Asia Minor to the ones he was controlling in Greece. Some of these city-states, being allies of Rome, screamed to high heaven, or rather to Rome, for help, which they got.

Philip was conquered by Titus Quinctius Flamininus, who was very popular among the Greeks, whom he had liberated, until they discovered that he was neither going to kill off Philip (especially not in the slow and grisly way some had hoped) nor loot Philip's cities and divide the booty with them. The Roman senate sent a panel of ten men to help Flamininus decide what to do with Greece. He concluded it should be set free if Roman honor was to be upheld and Roman sanity was to be preserved – dealing with the excitable Greeks was hard on sensible men.

The Greeks wept in joy and disbelief when they received their freedom and set about using it to do in their fellow Greeks.

Offering Flamininus any gift within their resources to show their gratitude, they were floored when he asked only for the freedom of all Italian slaves in Greece. Scratching their heads, they rounded these up and handed them over, muttering to each other that no right-thinking man would ever understand a Roman. The ancient Samnites, who had had to watch Dentatus spurning their gold for a dinner of turnips, could have sympathized.

Not every Roman was a Cato or a Dentatus, however, and all that Greek luxury and refinement, combined with the wealth that poured in after all those successful foreign wars, changed many a rustic Roman into a dandified city slicker. Cato's censorship, while it had scared the people it affected into some semblance of honesty, hadn't really changed the trend. When Lucius Aemilius Paullus defeated Perseus, the king of Macedon, in 167 BC, and allowed his sons to take only the king's books while the vast treasures of the king went into the public treasury, he was already out of step with the times. Scipio Africanus' daughter Cornelia might say that her two sons were her jewels but most Roman women of her class wanted something that complemented their best stolas better than a pair of unruly boys.

Those unruly boys of Cornelia's, Tiberius and Gaius Gracchus, were proud of a long family history of service to the republic.

Cornelia's Favorite Ornaments

Roman boys in the Good Old Days had grown up at their father's side, going to the field or the council hall along with him. They had even gone to the senate until they were excluded because an upstart mother tried to force her son to clue her in on the senate's closed-door deliberations.[7] As their father died when they were very young, the Gracchi would not have had such companionship anyway, but their strong-minded mother kept them well informed on the duties of the descendants of Scipio Africanus, BMOR.

Wealth was pouring in, the military commanders who brought it were treated as gods and the poor people, as usual, were getting shafted. As upper-class boys, the Gracchi should have adhered to the good old land-grab policies of the rich but instead, they took the side of the Populares. (Political parties along the old patrician vs plebeian lines were beginning to form. The *Populares*, or people's party, were the commoners; the *Optimates* or "Best" were the aristocrats. It is easy to see who named the parties.) Tiberius and Gaius wanted to give land to the poor people, many of whom had owned it anyway before Hannibal tramped around destroying crops for 16 years. They pointed out that not only did this plan have justice on its side but also it would reduce both the welfare rolls and the number of able-bodied loafers in Rome with nothing better to do than indulge in riots and crimes (sometimes simultaneously, sometimes separately). Unfortunately such clear-sighted and disinterested policies always manage to displease somebody who has his eye on a fast buck. To make matters worse, the Gracchi had that youthful impatience which wants sweeping changes made immediately, if not sooner. Any student of history could have told them that radical reformers usually don't live to collect their Social Security, and so it was with them. Although they had been legally elected to office, they were both murdered. These developments led thinking people to wonder if the good old civil system of obeying the officials that the people had elected hadn't sprung a leak. Indeed it had.

CHAPTER XV

"Ne, pueri, ne tanta animis adsuescite bella!"
Vergil, *Aeneid*, Book VI, 832

(Don't, boys, turn your hearts to civil war!)

Shortly after the death of the Gracchi, Gaius Marius, a young
Roman nobody (who didn't intend to remain one) had
impressed one of the great Metelli clan so much that he was taken
to Africa as senior legionary commander. This didn't keep him
from undermining Metellus and getting his command. He conquered the armies of the wily Numidian king, Jugurtha, and made
the mistake of parading Jugurtha through Rome as his catch when
the Numidian king had actually been bagged by young Lucius
Cornelius Sulla. From this point on relations between these two
ambitious climbers went from bad to worse, with Marius claiming
the loyalty of the Populares and Sulla that of the Optimates.

For the next 16 years or so they raised and trained their own
armies, defending Rome and expanding her power in between
bouts of slaughtering each other's adherents.

Marius was almost 20 years older than Sulla and one would
have thought old age and exhaustion would have removed him
from the lists, but he was made of hardy stuff. In 88 BC Sulla's
forces got the upper hand and Marius was declared a public
enemy (whether he was Public Enemy Number One is uncertain,
but likely). The vessel that was supposed to carry him to Africa,
meeting one of those Juno-type storms, found itself back on the
coast of central Italy. Its sailors, who had a well-honed if unheroic
sense of self-preservation, deserted the old man, who hid first in a
fisherman's hut and then in a swamp. In this latter refuge, he sank

in the mud up to his throat and was dragged forth and impris-
oned by the magistrates of the local town. When a slave was
dispatched to dispatch him with a sword, he found the muddy old
man in a dark (and now somewhat slimy) cell. Rising from his
earthy couch the old warrior thundered, "Would you kill Gaius
Marius?"[8] Even though the slave lacked modern educational
advantages and had never seen any Swamp Creature movies, he
took to his heels. Marius escaped to Africa to continue helping
Sulla create disaster.

The civil power was in shambles and half the populace either
dead, exiled, or impoverished, but these two loyal citizens went
right on dukeing it out until the aging Marius died in 86 BC.
Having used his army to wipe out a few leftover rivals from the
Marian period, such as Sulpicius and Cinna (along with any poor
soul he suspected of smiling on them), Sulla soon became dictator
and now, unhindered by Marius, he was able to go back to the
business of making everyone who was anyone miserable if they
displeased him. In this task he was ably abetted by two young
men who would be prominent in many coming disturbances –
Gnaeus Pompey and Marcus Crassus.

Sulla could be generous with his adherents but no one who had
seen the corpses piled around in odd spots could doubt his attitude when crossed. In spite of this, young Gaius Julius Caesar
flatly refused to divorce his wife at Sulla's command. Caesar had
married Cornelia, the daughter of the consul Cinna, whom Sulla
had sent to his eternal reward, and had furthermore committed the
grave sin of having an aunt who had married Marius. After young
Caesar stated his firm intention of remaining in his present marital
status, he wisely went East, where he remained until Sulla's death.

Chrysogonus, a freedman who was one of Sulla's more engag-
ing boon companions, had had a very wealthy man named Sextus
Roscius murdered, in conjunction with some of the man's poor
relatives. He then listed Roscius among Sulla's proscribed "traitors," so that his property could be confiscated. The poor relations
and Chrysogonus were preparing to divvy up the spoils when
they went too far – they accused the dead man's son of his murder.
Young Marcus Tullius Cicero, who was making quite a name for
himself as a legal advocate, defended young Roscius so well that

there was an acquittal and the whole plot was exposed. Cicero wisely took the position that Sulla was unaware of these dastardly deeds, but after young Roscius was acquitted Cicero still felt it was best to go to Greece for extended studies.

Sulla's abdication and death left Rome in yet another uproar, for Sulla had left his power to the senate, which was no longer fit to rule. Not only the citizens who wanted their rights back, but pirates on the sea and gangs of runaway slaves on land, roamed and robbed. The escaped gladiator Spartacus was perched on the volcano Mount Vesuvius, of all places, with a huge slave army, and soon marched forth to defeat armies and plunder the countryside. Crassus and Pompey between them finally sent him and his army to their grisly rewards. Crassus actually defeated them but Pompey decorated a few Roman roads with their crucified bodies and claimed the victory. This gave Crassus a life-long grudge against Pompey, which surfaced every once in a while, much to the delight of the senate. That august body, which had never recovered from its *rex* complex and always shuddered when confronted by a man of outstanding ability, reluctantly gave Pompey power over the seas. He finished off the pirates in style and then went to Asia Minor to flatten King Mithridates VI of Pontus. Matters were stabilized for the moment but the boiling tensions beneath the surface continued to bubble briskly.

CHAPTER XVI

"Catilina fuit magna vi animi et corporis sed ingenio malo."
Sallust, *Bellum Catilinae,* 1–2

(Catiline had great strength of mind and body but a
depraved spirit.)

While Pompey was strengthening his right to power in the East by the good old commander-with-an-army routine, Caesar, Crassus and Cicero were making their mark back in Rome. Crassus had not only his defeat of Spartacus but also his immense wealth to throw in the scale. Caesar had his relationship to Marius, his ancient lineage and his own great ingenuity, which had scarcely begun to surface yet. Cicero had his unmatched speaking ability.

A fourth "C," Lucius Catilina, who had been one of Sulla's less pleasant young friends, found his prospects drying up after Sulla's demise. Even after doing in his father-in-law and inserting his brother's name in the proscription list to raise money for his fun parties, he found himself still short of funds and was always having to borrow. He wanted to take over the country, plunder the wealthy and remit all debts, beginning with his own. Of course he did not announce this program when he ran for consul in 64 BC, but the senate had a fair idea of what he had in mind. Gritting their teeth, the senators supported Cicero, a *novus homo* (new man) who had risen from the merchant class, of all disgraceful places, by the power of his tongue.

Cicero was elected consul but Catiline did not take defeat gracefully. He got together some of his underworld cronies and made a plan for an armed uprising, the signal for which would be the murder of the consuls. Cicero, who had spies everywhere, naturally disapproved of this plan, and spilled it to the senate one morning instead of calling roll.

After Catiline left town as a result of his spoiled surprise, his deputies still in Rome, with breathtaking stupidity, wrote the whole plan out for some visiting Gauls whom they hoped to enlist. These Gauls had arranged with Cicero to be arrested once they had the goods.[9] The result was a hasty necktie party for the conspirators in Rome, some of whom were so powerful that Cicero feared that they would be rescued by their dependents if they stayed alive very long. In his necessary haste, however, he had overlooked the little fact that by law a Roman citizen must have a trial; he would pay for that later. Catiline and his rebel army in the hills were defeated. Catiline died fighting and Cicero had saved Rome – a fact that he never allowed anyone to forget.

Meanwhile Pompey returned, well aware of the services he had done the state on the seas and in the East, and found nobody was interested. A good general he was but a dull stick at a party and no good at flattering the masses.

Caesar, with his usual good sense, got himself elected Pontifex Maximus. This ancient title literally meant "Bridge Builder," and was given to a man who understood both the numbers and measures necessary to build a bridge and the omens and sacrifices that were supposed to keep the spirits from promptly dumping it into the river. In Caesar's day, the title belonged to the chief priest of all Roman religion. The mind might boggle at Caesar as high priest but the office had certain compensations – a salary and a lodging, as well as the fact that the priest was sacrosanct – no one could do him violence. (History would prove that last one wasn't worth much.)

Continuing his rise, as praetor Caesar backed the wrong aristocrat, Metellus Nepos, and had his office temporarily suspended. He was quickly restored to power, but before he could take the provincial governorship that was assigned to him at the end of his term, he ran into a bit of unpleasantness arising from the endless duel between Cicero and still another C – Clodius Pulcher.

This scion of the ancient house of Appius Claudius had all the energy, charm and general craftiness of his ancestors, but absolutely none of their civic spirit. He dabbled in politics from an early age, beginning with inciting the troops of his brother-in-law Lucullus to mutiny and continuing on a lively career of using his famous name to win over or to bludgeon Roman leaders, whichever offered a little profit for himself. He was just naturally a little bundle of fun and enjoyed stirring up cyclones by various pranks, one of which was disguising himself as a woman and sneaking into the festival of the Bona Dea.

The Bona Dea, or Good Goddess, was a deity worshipped exclusively by women, and all men were barred from her official nocturnal ceremony, which was held yearly in the home of the chief priest under the supervision of his wife. The chief priest was of course Julius Caesar and his wife, his beloved Cornelia having died, was Sulla's young granddaughter Pompeia. Clodius was not called Pulcher (Gorgeous) for nothing; he looked charming in his stola. Nevertheless, he was discovered in his woman's dress during the festival and the ladies turned him in amid much shrieking. Those who loved scandal said he could never have gotten in without a little help from his hostess, and wondered just what sort of persuasion he had used on her.

At Clodius' trial for sacrilege, Caesar refused to give evidence against him as the profaner of the ladies' festival. When asked why he had immediately divorced Pompeia, he loftily replied, "Caesar's wife must be above suspicion." When Clodius said with a great air of innocence that he had been a hundred miles from Rome on Festival Night, Cicero swore he had met Clodius on the streets of Rome that very afternoon. Clodius was acquitted, due to a huge bribe provided by Crassus, who was always trying to use his wealth to make himself a BMOR. Clodius swore revenge on Cicero. For this and other reasons, he persuaded the Roman Assembly to change his name from Claudius to Clodius, this giving him the status of plebeian and allowing him to run for Plebeian Tribune. When he got this office, he made some beautiful speeches about the sanctity (a word he should have blushed to use, except that he didn't know how to blush) of the law, and saw to it that Cicero was exiled for putting those henchmen of Catiline to death without a trial. It seems Caesar was smart simply to shed a wife who was at best dim-witted and at worst unfaithful, and otherwise to stay out of the whole affair.

As propraetor of the province of Further Spain, Caesar proved he could win both battles and the affection of soldiers and provincials, not to mention the affection of the common people.

The senate felt the *rex* complex stirring again, and to make matters worse, Pompey, Crassus and Caesar formed the First Triumvirate. Caesar invited Cicero to join them but that honor of Cicero's got in the way. Really, he was almost as bad as the younger Cato, the great-grandson of Cato the Censor, who was quite as big a killjoy as his ancestor.

La Dolce Vita **Gains Ground**

Cicero combined political savvy and idealism with a romantic view of the Senate As It Used To Be. True, Cineas the spokesman of Pyrrhus had called it "an assembly of kings," but that was in the Good Old Days. Far too many Stern Old Romans had been finished off by the various wars and far too many sons of Stern Old Romans had discovered *la dolce vita*. Caesar understood this, for he had few illusions about himself or anybody else. Cicero, on the other hand, was one of those unnerving individuals who build castles in the air and then energetically attempt to force a hapless real society to live in them. If such folk are influential enough, they rarely fail to gum up the works.

Things were moving along and soon Caesar was consul. In this position he ratified Pompey's treaties with the Near East countries and did other solid statesman-like things that the senate could possibly have forgiven. Some of his statesman-like deeds, however, they didn't like at all, such as making a strict law limiting the supplies that Roman governors could demand from the hapless provincials and forcing publication of senatorial transactions.[10]

Cato the Younger Killjoy had no quarrel with these laws but Caesar wanted to pass various measures Cato did disapprove of because they did not fit into the Grand Old Design of Rome As It Used to Be. As consul Caesar had to ask the senators strictly according to their rank, for their opinions of measures before the body. Unfortunately, like members of most political bodies, they could not be compelled to stay on the subject. When Caesar called for Cato's opinion on one particular measure, Cato talked on and on about everything he could think of so that the measure could not move forward. Caesar, tiring of this, had the sergeant at arms haul Cato, still talking, off to jail. The senate didn't like this high-handed behavior and followed Cato to his cell, listening much more attentively than they usually listened to him or to anybody else. Caesar gave up and ordered the release of Cato, who returned to the Senate House, still talking.[11] No doubt at this point lung power was established as the *sine qua non* for politicians.

After his consulship, Caesar was made proconsul, or governor, of Cisalpine Gaul and Illyria. The senate added Transalpine Gaul in the pious hope that if the Gauls didn't get him, the Germans would. As had happened so often in the preceding 50 years, the senate miscalculated badly. In his nine years in Gaul, Caesar would be, to say the least of it, successful.

CHAPTER XVII

"Gaius Julius Caesar noster, qui subiegit Galliam."
Song of Caesar's Legions

(Our Gaius Julius Caesar, who conquered Gaul.)

When Caesar arrived in Transalpine Gaul (Gaul-Across-the-Alps – from the Roman perspective, of course), he saw that his province there, which went by the highly original name of Province (and still does, only slightly misspelled in the French), was likely to be attacked. He reported this in his *De Bello Gallico* (Caesar felt that the best way to deal with the unreliable media was for a leader to write his own press releases – and mail them via his own messengers).

His northeastern neighbor was Helvetia (today called Switzerland, except on the coinage, which stills calls its state of origin by the jaw-breaking term Confoederatio Helvetica). Helvetia has the disadvantage, as Caesar hastened to point out, of being bounded on one side by the great river Rhine, which no one in his senses wanted to cross, since on the other side of that monstrous fluid fortification lurked the Germans; on another side by the Jura mountain range, one of the loftier segments of the Alps, across which were the unfriendly Sequani; and on the third by the gentle river Rhone, which was the boundary of Province. The Helvetians were 368,000 strong and most of their fields were perpendicular. They felt a great need of elbow room and it seemed that the best place to scoot somebody over was the Rhone.

Since, unlike many hopeful emigrants, the Helvetians were fully aware that the lands they coveted were occupied by people likely to resent being tossed out on their ears or other miscellaneous parts, they decided to go *en masse*. To be sure nobody lagged behind, they looted all fields and burned all dwellings. They then rode, walked and cursed their way toward the Rhone bridge at Genua. Their movements were not very fast and exceedingly obvious, so Caesar beat them to the bridge and by the time they got there the bridge was only a memory. They then politely sent envoys to Caesar, saying that they only wanted to cross his lands on the way to moving in on some unfortunate residents of Aquitaine. Caesar said he'd have to think about it; while he was thinking he had a wall and fortified ditch built from Genua to the Jura Mountains. Then he announced that he had decided not to let them pass and beat off all attempts to cross by force. The Helvetians went through a narrow pass in the Jura Mountains by treaty with the Sequani, and lumbered across south central Gaul. This set off a howl of protest from residents that could be heard all the way to Rome, with which some of those residents had treaties of alliance. The result was Caesar's Helvetian campaign, which brought victory and notoriety for him, more territory for Rome and a reduction of population for the Helvetians, of whom Caesar sent home 110,000 survivors after supplying them with food from Province. To senators insisting that they should be sold as slaves, he said that he needed a buffer state between Province and the Germans, who were seven feet tall and had blue eyes that could turn a man to ice when they looked at him.

This was the beginning of Caesar's Conquest of Gaul. Later on, some cities, such as Bratuspantium,[12] when they heard Caesar was coming simply sent envoys to surrender to him before he got there. He was a formidable enemy and had proved to be a generous overlord, so they felt they might just as well skip the formalities and get down to the foreign aid package.

Not everyone was so pacific in nature, however. The Germans had little interest in foreign aid and great interest in lands in Gaul. Caesar, who had a habit of referring to them as "the Germans, who live across the Rhine," thought it best that they remain *in situ*.

They kept venturing across the Rhine when it was in tranquil mood (or as tranquil as the Rhine ever gets) and trying to establish a little summer place. When these efforts failed they simply backtracked to the old homeland, feeling that no Roman with a brain would cross the widest, deepest and swiftest river known to them, a river which, according to their legends, could only be bridged by the gods. Caesar now showed that he was Pontifex Maximus in earnest, for he directed his engineers in building a bridge across the Rhine. He marched triumphantly across it and, having wreaked havoc and totally terrified the Germans for 18 days, recrossed the Rhine and destroyed the bridge. That settled the German Question for quite a spell.

Caesar also invaded Britain but he did not remain there long. Between storm, tides (which did not occur in the well-behaved Mare Nostrum), blue men (stained with a weed called woad) screaming down across the white cliffs of Dover, and the ever-restless Gauls at his back, Caesar had little time for properly organizing a Conquest of Britain. He made a few hasty notes on its strangest habits and returned to Gaul.

After nine years of triumphs and narrow escapes, Caesar had added to the Roman Empire an area almost one third of its size. Thanks to his tolerant policies, this area was loyal, not to Rome, but to Caesar. As he made his way south through Italy, being pelted with flowers by provincials and the Roman citizenry, the senate shuddered. They had never seen anybody who looked more like a rex.

CHAPTER XVIII

"Caesari omnia uno tempore erat agenda."
Caesar, *De Bello Gallico*, II, 20.

(By Caesar everything had to be done at the same time.)

Julia, the daughter of Caesar and the wife of Pompey, was a valuable link in keeping these two lions working together. But in 54 BC, with absolutely no consideration for her civic duty, she died. The senate had feared Pompey quite as much as it had feared Caesar, noting that he too had definite rex qualities, but for some time Caesar's success and popularity had united the senate and Pompey against him.

The senate ordered Caesar to disband his legions at the little Rubicon River, which marked the boundary between Cisalpine Gaul and Italy, and come into Rome alone. Caesar had a feeling that, given the senate's view of his activities, he was likely to meet with a sad accident before he reached the city, if he set out alone. Therefore, he entered Italy at the head of the sixth legion. As Caesar advanced south toward Rome, Pompey and his senatorial army, along with many senators who supported him, discovered that they had sudden business down in Brundisium.

Even if Caesar was no great mathematician, he had enough arithmetic to know that every time either side in a civil war killed a man, Rome was a soldier short. Thus, he was extremely reluctant to engage in civil war, being well versed in the horror stories from the time of Marius and Sulla. He had offered peace overtures to Pompey again and again without success. Now he went around the Empire defeating and pardoning the senatorial troops. Commenting on the fact that these pardoned fellows usually galloped right off to join another senatorial troop, Caesar said in a letter to Cicero, "They must be what they are; I must be what I am." A number of Romans would have been much happier if they had known what that was.

While all these stirring events were taking shape, Cato and Cicero, neither of whom was mentally deficient, had tried hard to stay out of a situation that promised destruction on all sides without any good results. As so often happens in such a fracas, however, thanks to their friends their good sense never had a chance. Both eventually were sucked into the vortex, although Cicero managed to wander around writing depressed letters for a long time before he committed himself to the losing side.

Finally, near Pharsalia in Thessaly, Caesar defeated Pompey in battle. Pompey rode hard for the coast and sailed to Egypt, where the young Pharaoh decided that his lifeless body would be a suitable present for Caesar. Caesar, who followed Pompey with a pardon, found that Pompey was in no state to listen to his offers.

After miscellaneous battles with various remaining forces, Caesar sailed to Africa, where the younger Cato was governing in Utica. Knowing his incorruptibility, Caesar had hoped to employ Cato in his new regime – perhaps as treasurer – but Cato belonged to that stern old Roman creed that had sent Lucretia, wife of

Caesar Enters Egypt

Tarquin Collatinus, looking for a suitable dagger. Having no faith in any rot about benevolent despots, he preferred to kill himself so that he could die with the Roman Republic. His suicide deprived Rome of an honest citizen, of which it already had a critically short supply. Perhaps it is just as well that most men fall lamentably short of Cato's resolution.

In July 46 BC Caesar returned to Rome and undertook many reforms, including an overhaul of the calendar, which certainly needed some help. Less than a year later he had to go to Spain and subdue Pompey's son, who made his father look like a saint – the most anti-Caesar politico shuddered at the thought of Young Pompey. Finally in September of 45 BC Caesar settled down to deal with such mundane affairs as overwhelming debt, bloated welfare rolls, footloose soldiers and malarial marshes. His excellent governing was interrupted on March 15, 44 BC by 23 stab wounds donated by the disgruntled senators who wanted to go back to the good old days of the republic, when all Romans were equal but senators were more equal than anybody else.

Rome was stupefied by Caesar's murder but it did not remain that way very long. It soon made its anger perfectly plain to the conspirators who had assassinated Caesar. This bewildered the conspirators, who had expected to be thanked for killing the man who was stabilizing Rome and for returning things to the bloody state of chaos that had existed before him. They decided to take up sudden residence in the Capitol and could not be tempted out of it for the senate meeting that Mark Antony, as consul and now ranking officer, set up. This complicated Roman owed his continued existence to the high-minded Brutus, who thought sinking a sword into his life-long friend and mentor (and according to the more gossipy traditions, his possible father) was a pious act of service to the gods, but that to add the blood of the debauched and unpredictable Antony might make the whole thing look like murder.

CHAPTER XIX

"Hic vir, hic est . . . Augustus Caesar, divi genus."
Vergil, *Aeneid*, Book VI, 791

(This is the man . . . Augustus Caesar, son of the deified.)

Young Gaius Julius Caesar Octavianus, Julius Caesar's great-nephew and adopted son, who was in an army camp over in Illyria, sailed quietly to Italy and learned that he was heir to Caesar's wealth and influence, both of which Antony was using as his own. All the common people of Rome and most of the provincials were howling for the assassins' blood, and none howled louder than Caesar's veterans, who rallied around Octavian.

Meanwhile back in Rome the senators had some problems. They hated to condemn the conspirators, who were their colleagues and who had their sneaking sympathy, as murderers. If they hailed them as deliverers, however, they had a raging mob of Romans just outside the Senate House to deal with and Antony hastened to remind them that such a hailing would render Caesar accursed and all his acts, by which everyone had benefited, null and void. Some of those whom Caesar had helped would not even be senators any more; many would lose their offices. Furthermore, that howling crowd of veterans outside would lose their benefits and create a catastrophe that was too horrible to contemplate.

The wily Cicero, who had not wasted his time in Greece, found the way out. In Old Athens a "forgetting" had sometimes been proclaimed; this meant that both sides agreed to forget the recent past and take no vengeance for it. (Political enemies still use this procedure after they have exhausted all possible means of doing each other in; it doesn't mean much today and it didn't mean much then, but it is a great way of getting past the moment.) That satisfied the senate, which was soon to learn that the ordinary Roman had little patience with such political refinements. The people's anger was red-hot and the public funeral oration the senate allowed Antony to give for Caesar stoked this fire, which needed no stoking. Antony reminded the people of all Caesar's mighty deeds and capped this moving speech by reading Caesar's will, in which he had left to each Roman a monetary gift from his fortune, equaling several weeks' wages. That did it. The conspirators fled for cover.

Realizing that Antony now held four aces, Cicero denounced him in a fiery set of speeches known as the Philippics, so named because the Greek Demosthenes had favored Philip II of Macedon with a similar set of uncomplimentary remarks. Cicero's influence went far to block Antony's power play and to force him to join forces with Octavian to flatten Caesar's assassins. When that was done, however, Antony would have plenty of venom left over for Cicero, who was eventually murdered by Antony's ruffians.

Meanwhile, Antony consistently underrated Octavian. He was slow to learn what Shakespeare, aided by 1,600 years of hindsight, makes a soothsayer tell him: "If thou dost play with him at any game, thou art sure to lose."[13] When Octavian arrived in Rome, he found that Antony was parading around Italy spending Caesar's money in an effort to win support. Octavian promptly began a series of public speeches promising to pay from his own money the legacy Caesar had promised if Antony squandered all Caesar's fortune. When Antony returned to Rome and treated young Octavian with contempt, the young man paid the legacies exactly as he had promised and won a host of friends. Moreover the senate, which saw *rex* printed on Antony's forehead and joined him in underestimating Octavian, welcomed the youngster as an ally. Octavian used the backing of the senate to help him force Antony to join him in destroying the murderers of his adoptive father, which was the first item on his extensive program.

The conspirators who had killed the now deified Julius Caesar had found it prudent to remove themselves from Rome. With Marcus Junius Brutus, descendant of the *pater patriae* Lucius Junius Brutus, and Gaius Cassius, a Pompeian who had been pardoned and honored by Caesar, at their head, they had set up headquarters in the East. Antony and Octavian led Julius Caesar's angry legions against them and the conspirators met their Waterloo at Philippi. After this victory, Octavian returned to Italy to raise money and Antony, ever the libertine, remained in the East to raise havoc. In this he was ably seconded by Queen Cleopatra of Egypt, who came barging up the river Cyndus to meet him dressed (using the term loosely) as Venus and simply dripping with gold and perfume. Two things that Antony admired in a woman were beauty and wealth, not necessarily in that order.

Cleopatra Barges up the Cyndus

Antony's intrepidity, or possibly his stupidity, was incredible, for he began an intrigue with Cleopatra and lingered in the East, even as his savage spouse, Fulvia, dressed in general's regalia and wearing a sword, waged war against Octavian. A thinking man with such a wife might have at least considered the pitfalls of infidelity.

Meanwhile Octavian made such progress in Italy that Antony, alarmed, returned to the Italian coast and was promptly refused admission by Octavian. Civil war would have been joined again, except that the soldiers, with good sense so seldom shown by their kind, flatly refused to fight. The result was a treaty. One wonders why future armies did not profit by this excellent example.

Under this treaty Antony, now a widower, married Octavian's sister Octavia. Octavia was one of those disconcerting Romans who lived up to and exceeded every ideal; her beauty, worth and intelligence charmed even the feckless Antony – for a while. Peace and prosperity for what was fast becoming the Roman Empire did not last long, however; Antony, becoming jealous of Octavian's power and popularity, began to long for Cleo and the old days of considering himself BMOR. The result was his return to Egypt and the Battle of Actium.

At Actium, Octavian defeated the forces of Antony and Cleopatra, and they both fled to Egypt for separate suicides. Octavian returned to a war-weary Rome as sole master of the world and sole survivor in the military head honcho sweepstakes.

He proceeded with great caution, remembering the unpleasant fate of Julius, and ceremoniously "restored the Republic." An exhausted senate threw in the towel, named him Augustus as well as Imperator, restored his powers and opened the doors of the Temple of Janus, indicating that the Roman world was at peace for the first time since a brief period after the First Punic War. War might be the natural state of humankind and peace an accidental interlude, but the Romans had had quite enough of the natural state for the moment. An accidental interlude of a couple of hundred years would be welcome.

CHAPTER XX

"Tu, Romane, memento pacisque imponere morem."
Vergil, *Aeneid*, Book VI, 851

(You, Roman, remember to impose the habit of peace.)

All the old Republican officials were still elected, although all were approved by Augustus, who was dutifully elected consul repeatedly and chose himself a co-consul. He finally asked from the senate the proconsular powers, which made him Big Daddy among rulers of provinces; from the Assembly he asked the tribunician powers, which gave him the veto and the right to initiate legislation and which set the death penalty for attacks upon his person (a knowledge of Roman history and the death of Uncle Julius made him a bit sensitive on this point). He also retained sole control of the army.

His efficiency in all things large and small made the senate – almost with a sigh of relief – turn even routine maintenance matters, which they had been bungling on a large scale, over to Augustus. After all, by this time the size and complexity of the Roman Empire was truly appalling. Conquering a vast empire is one thing; figuring out what to do with it, as Alexander the Great would have learned if he had lived long enough, is quite another matter. A governing body that had originated as the ruling organ of one city and its environs was hardly suited to handle such a huge and varied conglomeration of nations, even had that body been at its best, which the Roman Senate emphatically was not. The Roman Empire still lacked a few outlying sections, which it would acquire over the next century, but already it had bulged out in improbable directions, enfolding an incredible number of nations all bent on getting the upper hand of their neighbors. It required a shrewd overlord, who could organize a loyal and efficient civil service backed by a magnificent army, to keep it in any kind of order.

ROMAN EMPIRE
AT IT'S GREATEST EXTENT

A Conglomeration of Nations (AD 117)

The Roman economy received a double shot of vitamin B from the new security and the influx of Egyptian gold. The interest rate fell from twelve to four per cent; the economy was humming and the people were purring. Augustus settled down to rebuild and remoralize Rome, which after one hundred years of civil war needed a healthy dose of both activities. Excesses of all kinds, from bloodshed to sexual license, had rather run amok during the years of horrific or totally absent government. Restoring the ruined city was easy; restoring personal morals, as any religious reformer could have foretold, turned out to be a pony of a different hue.

Some years earlier Augustus had gotten off to a true Hollywood start by forcing Tiberius Drusus to divorce his pregnant wife Livia because he himself wanted to marry her. This romantic escapade set off a chain of events worthy of a Greek tragedy, as she had a young son by Drusus and was soon to bear another son. This second boy was widely rumored to belong to Augustus, although Tiberius Drusus claimed him. In an ordinary family such things could lead to a nasty amount of sibling rivalry; in the family of an empire ruler, the results were likely to be cataclysmic. For the moment, however, Augustus settled down with Livia to a simple life of living cleanly, governing wisely and avoiding extravagance. (Is it any wonder we have no movies set in this era?) His very clothes were woven by the women of his family. His daughter Julia, however, the product of Augustus' earlier marriage to Scribonia, preferred the way of life Augustus was trying to stamp out to the one he was trying to establish. She had no taste for weaving and a great taste for intrigue. Like most Roman women of noble birth she was destined to be married off to someone her father needed an alliance with; in fact, at the ripe old age of two she was betrothed to Antonius Antyllus, the son of Mark Antony and the lady-soldier Fulvia. The proposed wedding did not materialize, however, and Augustus reserved her for future political alliances. Young men of no great family who showed an interest in her received from the Imperator a letter that discouraged any further such folly.[14]

As soon as she reached a suitable age, Julia found herself married to Marcellus, Octavia's son, who was thus her cousin. When he died, depriving her of a husband and her father of an heir to power, she was married to Augustus' friend and supporter Marcus Agrippa. Agrippa was a contemporary of her father and after the young and charming Marcellus he probably wasn't exactly a heartthrob. However, Julia dutifully presented him with five children. As might have been expected, he died in a few years, and Julia, just home from the cremation ceremonies and barely settled into her widow's weeds, found herself betrothed to Tiberius, the disgruntled elder stepson Augustus had acquired through his sensational marriage. Both Augustus and Julia learned to detest Tiberius, who could be seen pouting around the palace because his family had been fractured and he thought nobody really loved him. Unloved he might have been but he became Imperator Number II just the same.

Augustus, by ruling unobtrusively and ably, managed to please most of the people most of the time so well that there was no serious attempt to overthrow him in his 44 years of absolute power. The Roman world released its pent-up breath, stretched and began to pursue the peaceful fleecing of neighbors by guile rather than by bloodshed.

Part of Augustus' restoration and remoralization program included artistic and literary works designed to appeal to the aesthetic sense of the Romans, which the ever-optimistic Imperator insisted was not totally ossified. Among others he enlisted the help of Maecenas, who may well have been unique among human beings – a man of wealth and a man of letters, devoid of personal ambition and devoted to his country. Encouraged by the patronage of Augustus and Maecenas, the Golden Age of Roman Literature flexed its muscles and got down to really serious business.

CHAPTER XXI

"Arma virumque cano."
Vergil, *Aeneid*, Book I, 1

(I sing of arms and the man.)

The Golden Age of Roman Literature had been going on, not
without its difficulties, during the civil wars. The last century
of the Roman Republic had inspired men to action and bloodshed,
but also to thought and speech, especially the latter. Men great
and small used high flights of language to get themselves out of hot
water or other poor souls into it. Cicero and Caesar in deathless
prose explained, condemned and defended myriad actions. The
Romans of the day were also enthusiastic correspondents; Cicero's
faithful freedman and secretary Tiro published 850 of Cicero's letters. Such an output of correspondence makes moderns wonder
how Cicero had time to do anything else. These letters give us
Cicero's view on everything and everybody in his day, including
and especially himself. Everybody is the center of his own universe
but Cicero did seem rather to carry this attitude to extremes. Not
the least annoying thing about him was that his boasts about his
prowess turned out to be true.

He was also a keen observer, not only of the political vagaries of
the day and his own excellence, but of the Roman scene. He was
unenthusiastic about large but mediocre theatrical offerings and
even more unenthusiastic about gladiatorial combats. He wrote
to his friend Marcus Marius complaining about the poor quality of
all the above entertainments at the opening of Pompey's theater in
55 BC. Reminding Marius that they both despised gladiators and
that no sensible man could enjoy the contests between man and
beast no matter which one won, he congratulated his friend on the

uncertain health that gave him an excuse for ignoring this whole extravaganza.[15]

Further light on his feelings in such matters is shed by his letter to his young friend Caelius, whom he had earlier defended from a trumped-up murder charge brought by the offended beauty Clodia. Caelius had been acquitted through Cicero's efforts and had gained the post of aedile. As he was now responsible for circus games, he wrote to ask Cicero for a different kind of help: he wanted a shipment of panthers from the province of Cilicia, of which Cicero was the governor. Cicero, at once refusing this request and patting himself on the back for his benevolent governorship, replied that the panthers had lodged a formal complaint because they alone were persecuted in Cicero's province, and in high dudgeon they had removed themselves from his province. Thus he was regrettably unable to supply his young friend with any animals for slaughter.[16]

All the above and much more literary activity went on without benefit of wealthy patrons. Obviously the need to separate one's neck as far as possible from the nearest executioner can be a powerful stimulant to literary creation.

Lucretius blamed everybody's problems on religion. Catullus, Propertius and Tibullus explored the pleasures and pains of love (Goethe, an extremely Romantic soul for a German, said that he preferred this Triumvirate to that of Caesar, Pompey and Crassus). While we are never sure how much of Propertius' and Tibullus' melancholy amours are real and how much just good theater, Catullus' path to true love actually was full of potholes. Coming to Rome as a very young man, he had the misfortune to meet Clodia, sister of Clodius Pulcher and descendant of all those Appii Claudii, none of whom had been known for their humility or gentle tempers. She was several years older than he, and she had spent those years merrily. Beautiful, clever and utterly heartless, she was the stuff *femmes fatales* are made of. Caesar might say she was the best woman in Rome to stay away from, and Cicero might call her "the very good friend of all men,"[17] but these gentlemen were getting on in years.

Catullus saw her in a very different light. He began in matchless poetry to celebrate the woman he called "Lesbia." He used this pseudonym to compare Clodia to the great Greek poet Sappho who had lived on the island of Lesbos. He felt a pseudonym was necessary because he did not want to embarrass her when he read the poems aloud in public. The poor innocent did not realize that few things, least of all compliments, were likely to embarrass Clodia. After a stormy and mostly unhappy love affair, Catullus died at the age of thirty, evidently from a combination of illness, malnutrition and utter despair. Some writers say he was the first, and in all probability the last, Roman to die for love.

Many smoother and lengthier effusions were to be written and preserved in the quieter times of Augustus, when one had leisure to withdraw to a farm not under siege and ponder one's dactylics. A writer might even be rewarded with gold rather than with just a stay of execution should his work be outstanding. Maecenas offered generous patronage to those writers whom Augustus hoped would reconstruct the eroded Roman character through great literature.

Both Maecenas and Augustus were fortunate in that within the usual crowd of needy poets lurked Vergil, Horace and Propertius. All three of these men had become at least somewhat needy through the massive confiscations of property, which took place while Augustus was rewarding his victorious veterans. Horace had even fought briefly for Brutus and the conspirators, but he says himself that he was the world's worst soldier, hiding under a bush at the first sign of disaster. Possibly Augustus thought that Horace had been of more use to him in the opposing army than in his own. Certainly he held no grudges for the past; soon Horace was pardoned and became a member of the circle of Maecenas, to which the generous, unworldly Vergil, totally lacking in professional jealousy, had introduced him. Among Horace's works is a set of songs celebrating the gods and the achievements of Augustus, commissioned by Augustus of course, and written for the Ludi Saeculares of 17 BC.

Propertius (who had managed to last into the Augustan age) had grace and wit, but was not overflowing with Good Old Roman Patriotism. He was very little help in rebuilding Rome, preferring to rebuild over and over again his relationship with a Jezebel he called Cynthia.

Propertius Rebuilding

Vergil was the crown jewel of Maecenas' brilliant circle. Because of his demonstrated talent, this shy and quiet man was assigned the task of writing a national epic to restore the self-esteem and patriotic fervor of Rome. Taking the trials of Aeneas as his text, he succeeded so well that he, like Byron, "awoke to find himself famous." He did not take to notoriety nearly so well as Byron did, and sometimes fled from his fans to hide in the nearest house. His dying wish was that the *Aeneid* should be destroyed because he had not perfected it. Augustus, knowing full well who was boss around there, ordered it to be published instead. Scholars through the ages have had a wonderful time discovering the parts of the *Aeneid* that need polishing but it remains one of the world's great literary works.

Maecenas and his poets notwithstanding, Augustus also

encouraged the historian Livy, who in 142 books set forth Everything That Had Ever Happened in Rome. Only 35 of these books now exist and Latin students struggling with translation have a hard time feeling really sorry about the loss.

Ovid, like Catullus, really didn't fit the Roman persona. Catullus had died for love, of all ridiculous notions, and Ovid, to the shame of his ancestors, liked to play. When the Romans sinned, they usually did it with a solemn lustiness. Ovid just couldn't stop laughing and, worse yet, poking fun at himself and his fellows. One morning he woke to find himself exiled to Tomi, a dreary little Roman outpost on the edge of the Black Sea, where the cultured debaucheries of the Rome he knew were conspicuously absent. He ascribed Augustus' banishment of him to a poem and a mistake. The poem was probably his *Art of Love*, which hadn't helped at all with Augustus' moral reforms; scholars have lots of fun speculating on the mistake. One of the juicier speculations involves an intrigue with Augustus' scandalous daughter Julia; some of the duller ones involve revolution plans. A few ambitious

Ovid Enjoying Life at Tomi

scholars have combined the two. However that may have been, Ovid remained in his one-mule town, begging to come home, until he died some time after Augustus did. With his death the Golden Age of Roman Literature gave up the ghost, to be replaced by the stupendous efforts of a group of writers who had no idea that they were to be forever labeled Writers of the Silver Age of Roman Literature, or Second Best.

CHAPTER XXII

"Prima inter urbes, divum domus, aurea."
Ausonius, *Opuscula*, Book XI, 1

(First among cities, home of the gods, golden Rome.)

Augustus ruled the world very well but like other great rulers he had little success ruling his family. Not only had he no sons, and only one daughter who scarcely shared his ideas on the simple life, but the sons his daughter and sister produced,who should have made good successors to the Imperator, kept dying. Since an heir to Roman power usually spent his formative years on the battlefield, a certain amount of attrition was to be expected, but far too many of these prospective rulers died of odd diseases. The Pontine Marshes near Rome (which Julius had intended to drain before he got mixed up with that set of busybodies waving daggers) were still busily turning out germs of many descriptions, so perhaps the odd diseases might also have been expected. But so much of the best Roman blood had been spilled in power intrigues that people just naturally looked at the latest corpse and cried, in the manner of Cicero, *"Cui bono?"* or "Who got a promotion out of this?"

At last Augustus was forced to adopt his stepson Tiberius as his heir, especially since his younger brother Nero Claudius Drusus (whom Augustus favored and whom the nasty-minded believed to be Augustus' son) had died on the German frontier. Augustus had earlier forced Tiberius to divorce his wife Vipsania and marry Augustus' daughter Julia, an arrangement that brought lasting satisfaction to absolutely nobody. Even though Tiberius had a son of his own, Augustus now forced him to adopt Germanicus, the son of his late younger brother, as his heir apparent. Perhaps this was good for Rome, but it did very little for family harmony.

Germanicus was commander-in-chief of the Roman forces in the Gallic and German provinces. Handsome and idealistic, with a quick sword in battle and a kindly word for the wounded in the field hospital, he was adored by everybody, with the possible exception of his uncle Tiberius. From Augustus down to the lowest soldier, Romans made no secret of their belief that Tiberius was totally unnecessary in the scheme of things. As this did nothing to sweeten his surly temper, the stage was set for Tiberius' gloomy reign and the mind-boggling family alliances and enmities, which we shall shortly discover dominating the rest of the reign of the Twelve Caesars.

While all this was going on in the palace, the Roman world was breathing deeply and reveling in the Pax Augusta, which would expand into what is often called the 200-year Pax Romana, arguably the longest period of peace ever enjoyed by so large a section of the world. The Pax Romana was by no means a total absence of war but, according to some rhapsodic poets near its end, a period when a great overseeing government generally sought the welfare of the general populace, allowing many peoples to go about life's business safely under its wide umbrella. Life in Augustus' Rome had many advantages, which ranged from the simple absence of street warfare to a newly-beautified capital city. Augustus had boasted that he had found Rome a city of brick and left it a city of marble. This was much closer to the truth than such boasts usually are.

A city of marble it might be but there was plenty of wood and other flammables under, behind and between the marble columns and slabs. Back in the Bad Old Days of the late republic, Marcus Licinius Crassus, playmate of Pompey and Julius Caesar, had organized a fire brigade of 500 lusty slaves. When a building caught fire, Crassus' brave firefighters had rolled up, held off any energetic citizens bent on aid or salvage, and watched while Crassus dickered with the owner of the fast-disappearing building over its purchase. Plutarch, who may be prone to occasional exaggeration, says that most of Rome had come into his hands in this way. Augustus put an end to this novel form of private

The City of Brick becomes a City of Marble

enterprise by organizing a core of *vigiles*, or watchmen, who took a more public-spirited attitude toward putting out a fire.

Augustus dealt successfully with many problems, but he had no luck in arresting the falling birthrate. Whatever else an all-powerful ruler can force people to do, in trying to make them have children and raise them he is likely to stub his toe. Augustus enacted laws to the advantage of married people who had three children and to the disadvantage of the unmarried and the childless, but the Romans, having added up the expenses of child-rearing and balanced them against the tax break, went right on having as few of the little busters as possible. Wars, executions and disease added to the problem.

On top of all this was the Romans' absolutely morbid penchant for suicide. As Lucretia had shown at the birth of the republic,

Romans preferred doing themselves in to a variety of survivals they considered disgraceful. While the fearful regimes of the Imperators after Augustus would be filled with gruesome demises, and some of the best and strongest Romans would have their blood spilled for them by these idiots, many would spill their own blood. The nastier-minded rulers to come would order powerful men they feared to commit suicide. Wives, daughters and other relatives would commit suicide in sympathy with a condemned loved one. This may have demonstrated family loyalty, but it didn't do much for family continuity. Julius Caesar by his pardons had tried to arrest the gradual disappearance of Romans and we all know how that turned out. Augustus with his tax breaks tried to reverse the continuing trend, but he didn't have much success either.

Augustus' death and Tiberius' ascension to power, brought about only after an embarrassing debate in the senate, seemed to the Roman legions in the North excellent excuses to revolt and declare Germanicus Princeps, Imperator, or whatever the absolute ruler was now calling himself. Germanicus would have none of this; he hastened to put down the revolt and swear allegiance to his uncle. Tiberius believed that this Germanicus For Princeps movement had support in Rome and a round of prosecutions and persecutions of the powerful people at Rome followed, while Germanicus was subduing the ever-rambunctious North.

Germanicus' loyalty didn't impress Tiberius very much; he had long ago decided that everybody hated him and he wasn't about to abandon a cherished belief now. Always a forbidding and grim personality, Tiberius had been well aware that Augustus had disliked him from childhood. After all, since in the Imperator's will were the words "since an unkind fate has robbed me of my grandsons, I make Tiberius my heir," Tiberius could be pardoned for feeling a bit unloved. While he had painstakingly carried out every duty assigned to him competently, even the doddering youngster Claudius, Germanicus' younger brother, often received more genuine kindness from Augustus. The gossip-mongers had snickered that Augustus was honoring the Blood of the Caesars, however addlepated. When Germanicus showed him family respect Tiberius suspected duplicity from this grandson of Mark Antony who might be a grandson of Augustus as well.

Back on the northern frontier Germanicus was soldiering on. During the seesaw wars with the Germans a rumor reached Germanicus' camp that he and his army had been destroyed, like the luckless Roman general Varus and his troops a generation before. The terrified garrison, remembering all those skulls of Romans nailed to various trees, rushed to break down the bridge over the Rhine, which was the only approach to camp either for the expected German attack or for the returning Romans. The Romans leaving camp screeched to a halt when they discovered Agrippina, the wife of Germanicus, who was in the war camp with her children, coolly standing in the middle of the bridge and daring them to break it down. This daughter of Agrippa and Augustus' daughter Julia had all the courage, resourcefulness and crusty cussedness of her ancestors. Soon the Roman army, which happened to be victorious, returned. The shamefaced Romans in camp gave thanks for the return of their beloved leader, and the Germans gave thanks that Agrippina did not choose to lead the armies.

Tiberius, for reasons of his own, decided to call Germanicus home, separate him from the northern legions that loved him, and pack him off to Asia Minor. There Germanicus showed to the nations of the East the courtesy and interest in everyone's well-being that seemed natural to him, even while he set up two new Roman provinces. Tiberius helped out by making Gnaeus Piso governor of Syria so that he could keep an eye on Germanicus. This unpleasant individual was widely suspected of poisoning Germanicus at Tiberius' request. Since Germanicus had recently been traveling in Egypt, his wasting away could have been brought about by almost anything he ate, drank, inhaled, or, according to the legends, said or did to offend the 5,000-year-old collection of grisly spirits that desert land harbors. Neither Germanicus nor his family, however, blamed Egypt for his illness; they saw Tiberius' fine Italian hand in the whole situation. Germanicus died calling upon family and friends for vengeance, which they promised with enthusiasm.

A grieving empire and a hysterical city responded to Germanicus' death with an excess of grief that Tiberius promptly censured. Agrippina, the widow of Germanicus, was as formidable

A Formidable Helpmeet

a partisan of his memory in death as she had been of his safety in life. She believed that Tiberius had destroyed him so that the Blood of the Caesars would never again rule Rome, and she set about in a series of machinations that Lady Macbeth might have envied, to rally senatorial support against the Imperator. She succeeded so well that Tiberius, who had a depressing and perhaps well-founded conviction that most of the people around him were trying to do him in, had her exiled and then starved to death. (Of her nine children, four outlived her – one of whom Rome would have the bad luck to inherit as the emperor Caligula.)

Meanwhile Tiberius was taking good, and sometimes too good, care of the Empire according to his extremely conservative views. A medieval historian says that a man sought audience with Tiberius to show him a new invention. The man entered the Presence bearing a beautiful glass goblet, which he proceeded to hurl to the floor. The glass did not break, but dented. The inventor then beat it out with a small mallet and handed it, good as new, to the Imperator. "Does anyone except yourself know the secret of this glass?" asked Tiberius. Upon the inventor's assuring him proudly that the secret was his alone, Tiberius ordered him executed to preserve the price of precious metals.[18] Even for Economic

Protectionism this seemed a little extreme and it went a long way to discourage research and invention.

While Tiberius was ruling Rome and making an amazing assortment of enemies, he was a perfect example of the truism "a boy's best friend is his mother." (Later Nero would prove that a mother's best friend is not necessarily her boy.) Livia far outlived Augustus, dying in AD 27 at the age of 85. She had received the title of Augusta and wielded immense influence. In this age of dying Caesars the lovers of scandal of course hinted that she had had a hand in Tiberius' position as Almost Sole Survivor, but sadly there is no evidence of this to furnish Hollywood with some nice juicy plots. In AD 23, however, the province of Asia, which was never at a loss for hair-raisingly bizarre ideas, showed its awareness of her power when it sued for permission to erect a temple to a unique trinity: Tiberius, his mother Augusta, and the Roman senate.[19]

As Tiberius' sullen nature was spotlighted more and more, Romans of every class grew to hate him, and he withdrew to the Isle of Capri to sulk, leaving the Roman Empire largely in the hands of an extremely competent civil service and an incredible schemer named Sejanus, who would have fitted nicely into a modern horror novel. Sejanus, a mere Roman knight with no smattering of noble blood, intended to be the next Imperator, and with that end in mind set about systematically destroying Tiberius' close relatives. He should have known that no real plot could escape the suspicious mind of Tiberius, who fancied a traitor under every bush. All Rome rejoiced with good reason when Sejanus was trapped in his own plots and condemned to be strangled.

Tiberius hauled Gaius Caligula, the surviving son of Germanicus and Agrippina, off to Capri with him. The boy had noticed that open opposition to Tiberius had led his mother to a sticky end; he learned to conceal his hatred of the man who had destroyed his family and developed a life-long ability to smile sweetly while plotting nasty revenges. On Tiberius' death, Germanicus' addlepated brother Claudius being ignored, Caligula became Imperator. Rome soon realized that this scion of the Caesars had more than one tile missing from his roof. After numerous attempts at assassination someone finally succeeded in killing him. His stultified uncle Claudius, whom a soldier found hiding behind a curtain, was proclaimed Emperor by the army while the senate was discussing a restoration of the republic. Once again long-winded discussion had proved the senate's undoing.

The human race generally shows a preference for the handsome and well spoken, however great rascals they may be; shy folk who stammer and suffer from some type of palsy are usually not considered suitable candidates for high office. Everyone who mattered had long since decided that Claudius was a twig on the family tree best ignored. He had lived quietly in the country, studying literature and history and writing learned books in both Latin and Greek, for most of his life. To some this was even more appalling than his physical defects.

As Imperator he unfortunately inserted the wisdom he had gained into long and incredibly dull speeches in the senate, during which Roman senators often enjoyed the most restful snoozes they had had in years. He took his duties seriously, however, and devoted so much of his time to a real effort at good administration that he had to confine the gambling, of which he was extremely fond, to his large traveling carriage, which was fitted with gaming equipment.

His greatest achievement was the conquest of Britain, which Augustus and Tiberius had said would be too expensive. Conquering this island was desirable, as it was a great source of tin and also a great source of Druidism, a nature religion that sometimes featured Roman prisoners as bloody offerings under sacred oak trees.

As the battle for Britain got hotter, Claudius himself arrived, complete with war elephants, which created quite as big a sensation in Britain as they had in Italy in the Old Days of Rome. One's first elephant seen in a circus is bad enough; on a battlefield it tends to produce extreme coldness of the feet. In spite of the elephants, it took four years to conquer most of present-day England, after which the Romans, like many peoples after them, would waste a lot of time trying to subdue permanently the Welsh and the Scots.

Claudius was a perfect example of "uneasy lies the head that wears the crown." He ingratiated himself with absolutely nobody, and fell prey to the machinations of Agrippina the Younger, daughter of Germanicus and Agrippina. This redoubtable lady possessed all her mother's facility in intrigue, and she persuaded poor Claudius to marry her. (This took a special dispensation from the senate, as, however desperate for children Rome might be, the marriage of an uncle and a niece was frowned upon.) After this, she maneuvered him not only into adopting her frightful son Nero but into appointing Nero guardian of Claudius' own young son Britannicus. Anyone even slightly acquainted with the dour conviction of Germanicus' family, that he and therefore they themselves, had been cheated of the right to rule could have foreseen a short life for both Claudius and Britannicus. Indeed it seemed that by some grim joke of the gods all the wrong Caesars survived.

All the Wrong Caesars Survived

In the fullness of time, Agrippina the Younger duly shepherded Nero onto the throne to fulfil the thwarted destiny of his family, as he was descended not only from Germanicus and Augustus through her but from Mark Antony through his father. This father, who was well aware that not all the qualities of the Caesars and the Antonys were admirable, reportedly said that only evil could be expected of a son of his and Agrippina's. His son lost little time in proving this prophecy true. At first his abominations were committed only against literary sensitivity. According to contemporary accounts, Germanicus had penned some pretty respectable writings; Nero, in this area as in so many others, tried and abysmally failed to ape his illustrious ancestor.

When Nero became Imperator at seventeen, Agrippina fully intended to rule while he amused himself with wine, women, song or whatever else took his fancy. She had reckoned without Afranius Burrus, commander of the Praetorian Guard, and Seneca, Nero's tutor – two sensible men whom she herself had chosen to educate and protect Nero. They quietly undermined her influence with the youngster and kept the empire running smoothly; Nero had no objection to good government, provided it didn't interfere with his artistic endeavors. Several years passed prosperously until the evil day when Nero set his sights on the beautiful Poppaea Sabina. She set out to become his wife and her first step in this campaign was to goad him into killing his mother. This murder was accomplished, though with difficulty; Agrippina kept escaping the accidents carefully planned for her. When she was finally dispatched, both Seneca and Burrus intervened to protect Octavia, Nero's wife, whose future did not look promising, but on the death of Burrus, Seneca was driven into exile. Octavia was divorced and Poppaea had won – for the time being. There was, however, some measure of morbid justice in her death; legend says she died of a kick administered by her loving husband in a fit of rage.

Nero's most successful years as Imperator had been spent under the guidance of Seneca but he murdered this philosopher along with quite a hefty slice of Roman society. Nero was probably innocent in the matter of the great fire that destroyed most of Rome in 64 AD. He was most certainly not fiddling, as the violin would not be invented for a thousand years or so. However, since the Romans had long ceased to believe that he could be innocent in any matter, things looked dangerous.

Tacitus says that Nero decided to blame this conflagration on the Christians, who had gathered to themselves all the unpopularity natural to a group of Puritans preaching in a sin-loving world. Nero murdered Christians in all the bizarre ways he had developed while practicing on pagans, and sensible men throughout Rome felt he badly needed replacing. The Roman legions began to raise candidates on every hand, and Nero fled from the city. The senate gave orders for his capture and execution, and the world sighed with relief when Nero, with some help from a loyal freed-man, managed to commit suicide. The reign of the Julio-Claudians, Caesars by blood, had come to an end, thank goodness. These last ones might have been descended from Julius and Augustus, but it was clear that the line had descended a long way.

CHAPTER XXIII

"Puto deus fio."
Said by the Emperor Vespasian when dying

(Oh-oh! I think I'm becoming a god.)

Nero's death was followed by the Year of Four Emperors, which gives us some idea of the chaotic state of things. During Nero's turbulent last days, the Roman legions in Spain had backed Galba, the elderly governor of Hither Spain, while the Rhine legions backed Verginius Rufus, who with admirable good sense refused the honor. Imperator Galba soon got himself murdered, as did the three who followed him in rapid succession.

When the noise abated a trifle and the blood was mopped up, the dour soldier Vespasian was Imperator in every sense of the word. The Caesars were no more and the Flavians had arrived; Vespasian celebrated this event by taking to himself the title "the Caesar."

He might be the son of a tax collector, but Titus Flavius Vespasianus had dynastic ideas and insisted that his power should be inherited by his sons. In the meantime, however, he vigorously exercized it himself. He and his son Titus had dealt quite competently with Palestine before he became Emperor; he now dealt with Germany and Gaul efficiently also. Vespasian revoked the hated "treasonable speech" laws: he didn't care what people said; it was actions, not speeches, that concerned him. Like Augustus he lived simply; the gossipy historians Tacitus and Suetonius insisted that his one vice was his rigid thriftiness. Indeed his ideas on economy would have put a Scot to shame.

Vespasian resembled Augustus in another respect – he had a

ravaged Rome and a recalcitrant Empire on his hands. His tax-collector blood came to the fore, and the people found to their disgust that he had a genius for assessing value and collecting on it. No tax collector could cheat him and he didn't even squander the profits in visible debauchery. He used some of the money he collected and saved to create an endowment for professors, which was so radical that even jaded Rome was shocked: whoever heard of an Imperator spending good money on education? He was a sore disappointment to the people because he gave them absolutely nothing to gossip about; they had long since forgotten how to deal with a sensible Imperator. He restored stability and scorned pretense, laughing at those who wanted to construct an impressive pedigree for him and scoffing, as he neared death, at the idea of deification.

Like Tiberius, Vespasian believed in Economic Protectionism. Suetonius tells of an engineer who offered to haul some huge columns up the Capitoline Hill at moderate expense using a device of his own invention. Not resorting to Tiberius' extreme measures, Vespasian paid the engineer handsomely but refused his services, saying that he must be sure that the working classes earned enough money for food. One wonders if the poor properly appreciated his preservation of their backbreaking jobs.[20]

Vespasian worked hard as Imperator; according to the elder Pliny, he worked several hours and then slept one, winding up with about 4 hours' sleep out of 24. Counselors and government officials could be seen yawning as they stumbled into the imperial offices at all hours. Legend says that at the age of seventy Vespasian died standing, as he said an Imperator should die, hard at work to the end. A few more rulers like him might have taken all the glamour out of cheating, lying and murdering in order to get to the top.

On Vespasian's death, his son Titus inherited the power, but he certainly didn't work 20 hours of the day. Neither of Vespasian's sons was comparable to their father, but Titus didn't live long enough to become unpopular. The only major event during his reign was the eruption of Mount Vesuvius, for which not even the senate could blame him. He won popularity by succoring the victims of the eruption and by completing the Flavian

Amphitheater, which everyone began calling the Colosseum because of its nearness to the Colossus, a huge golden statue of himself which Nero had erected to enhance the beauty of the city.

When Titus, still handsome and popular, died in the second year of his reign, his baby brother Domitian rose to the throne. Domitian had neither the good sense of his father nor the good looks of his brother. He had not been a soldier like Titus and Vespasian; he had absolutely no credits to place in his resume. Vacillating and vain, he was the kind of specimen that gives baby brothers a bad name; soon Rome was whispering that he had poisoned Titus. This cheery bit of gossip did not improve his vicious outlook. He not only restored the "treasonable speech" rules, but also shared the treasures of rich men with anyone who could bear witness that they had spoken against him. He sent his cousins Flavius Sabinus and Flavius Clemens to execution, the first on the usual charge of treason, the second because he and his wife had embraced a foreign religion. Tradition says that the home of Flavius Clemens was a Christian meeting place – the lowest level of the three-level Church of San Clemente in Rome. The Christians were up to their old tricks of censoring everybody's nasty little pleasures, and Domitian thought that they, along with a sizeable number of perfectly good pagans, should be eliminated, especially if they were attracting noble Romans with their Puritan notions.

During Domitian's last years, he dreaded assassination and walked always in a corridor lined with mirrors so that nobody could sneak up on him. Everyone went in fear of him, with the usual result – somebody murdered him.

The conspirators who did Domitian in had already selected a successor, the elderly and gentle senator Nerva. His reign was short, and he really wasn't good for much except that he selected as his successor the great Trajan, who had all the skills and strength Nerva lacked.

CHAPTER XXIV

"Salus populi suprema lex esto."
Cicero, *De Legibus*, III, 3

(Let the safety of the people be the supreme law.)

Now we come to a time on which Hollywood is generally silent, which indicates that Rome finally got a break. The reigns of the Four Good Emperors don't attract the ghoulish; film producers only find interesting two facets of the last parts of this peaceful period – the possibility that Marcus Aurelius was murdered and the subsequent reign of his appalling son Commodus.

The first of the Four Good Emperors was Trajan, who was assisted, for a change, by a family that was loyal to him. His was an old Roman family, which had been established in Spain since the times of Scipio Africanus, quietly going about its business and not practicing any interesting perversions, which explains why we have never heard of them. A thoroughgoing and practicing Stoic, Trajan believed that duty was supreme and that, as Imperator, his duty was to see to the welfare of the people. He has always been a severe disappointment to people who believe that the first qualification for being Imperator of Rome was the mental stability of a mud-puddle. In a shocking break with recent policy, he considered even the rich and the well-born to be people who deserved a chance to live without harassment. Among his friends were those worthy men nobody ever made a fortune writing about – old-fashioned Romans such as Pliny, philosophers such as Epictetus and orators such as Dion Chrysostom – Dion of the Golden Tongue. After a brief acquaintance with Domitian, this scholarly orator had not surprisingly become a Cynic and had wandered the world staff in hand, trying to persuade people to temperance and justice. Such activity produced little improvement in human behavior, but it developed his speaking abilities amazingly. Dion was often invited to dine and to travel with Trajan, who said of his more learned orations, "I don't understand a word of them but I love his beautiful speech."

One of Trajan's able assistants was Pliny the Younger, whom Trajan sent to govern the feckless province of Bithynia, which certainly needed governing, guiding, spanking or something it wasn't getting. The Bithynians were in the habit of applying for public funds to build needed town improvements such as aqueducts, granting contracts to their friends to build said improvements, and then discovering that the money had somehow managed to melt away and leave them with a half-finished aqueduct, which usually fell down. Pliny's first move amazed the Bithynians: he sent to Rome for engineers who actually knew how to build structures such as aqueducts. Next, exhorted by Trajan in very strong language, he set out to find out who had been responsible for the earlier adventures in expenditure.

As a man with an eye to engineering advances, saving resources and keeping a few extra *denarii* in his own pockets, Pliny was a good choice for streamlining feather-headed provinces. In his two country villas he had employed, among other modern advances, the solar heating techniques advocated by Vitruvius. His houses were built so that transparent panels of glass or mica, a novelty commented on by Seneca, would collect the sunlight in certain rooms and save both heating bills and natural resources. Pliny was a very rich man and he intended to remain one.

This careful governor soon discovered that the Byzantines (who lived in the city that would one day be overwhelmed by Constantine's desire for a new capital – named after himself, of course) were spending a king's ransom each year to send a special envoy to Rome to present their homage to the Imperator. Pliny instructed them simply to put a nice note in the post he was sending to the Imperator anyway and skip the special envoy.

Pliny also encountered some of the outlawed Christians. He dutifully reported to Trajan that on careful examination he had found them guilty of nothing worse than gathering before daylight every seventh day, singing some perfectly awful songs, and promising that for another seven days they would go against human nature by refusing to steal from their friends or indulge in crime. While it might be weird, Pliny did not think such behavior was actually subversive and Trajan accepted his opinion.

Pliny, like his idol Cicero, was an orator of grace and polish, but even under so generous an Imperator as Trajan there was little scope for such talents in the political sphere. Cicero had won fame by swaying the senate's decisions and winning acquittal for those falsely accused of crimes. In Pliny's day these matters were decided with a sharp eye on Imperial opinion. Civil cases, though, were another matter. In these there was room for oratory in such suits as the one decided by the jurist Ulpian in Pliny's own century. Ulpian heard the case of a fuming plaintiff who, like Pliny, owned a *heliocaminus*, or sunroom. The plaintiff's neighbor had built a structure that blocked the sunlight from that sunroom, and Ulpian decided said structure would have to go. His decision was recorded in the Law Code of Justinian four centuries later.[21] After all, what kind of a country is it if a man can't defend his own *heliocaminus*?

After a reign of 18 years or so, Trajan did something rare among Roman Imperators – he died peacefully of a simple illness. On his deathbed Trajan adopted as his successor Hadrian, whose father was his first cousin. At least Trajan's wife Plotina said he had adopted Hadrian and Trajan was in no state to deny it. Hadrian, who had been a favored and hardworking commander under Trajan, became an exemplary Imperator. If his adoption was a falsehood, it was the most fortunate falsehood in the history of Rome.

Like Trajan, his successor Hadrian scarcely provided a subject for sensational and financially rewarding biographies. He defended, restored and fortified cities and states, helped the people and punished criminals. He ended the horrendous old system of tax farming, in which the Roman government hired a local collector to collect and turn over to them the assessed taxes of an area. As the collector generally kept on squeezing the people long after he had collected what he sent to the Romans, obviously there was room for improvement. A professional civil service, answerable to

A Well-Chosen Heir

the Imperator, brought about improved finances for both the tax-payer and the government.

Hadrian's gravest fault may have been being too helpful. He set up such exact instructions for every occupation high or low that people learned simply to follow the guidelines and gave up the fatigue of thinking for themselves or improving standard methods.

This Imperator, unlike the ones whose character had been only too easy to read, was an enigma. A confirmed skeptic, he preserved the temples of the ancient gods and dabbled in astrology. An able soldier and a good architect, he indulged in such shameful practices as painting and writing poetry. He traveled through the Empire, which by this time took some doing, living roughly or elegantly as occasion warranted and exploring exotic places. He even took his wife Sabina, who seems to have been no great favorite of his, for a merry sail on the Nile.[22] Perhaps, though, going along on this particular expedition was her idea. Remembering the long-dead Cleopatra, perhaps Sabina was taking no chances on the kind of havoc an Egyptian queen could wreak.

Hadrian returned to Rome in the grip of a painful illness and, having no children, looked about him for a suitable replacement. He adopted Lucius Verus and bestowed on him the title of Caesar, which hereafter would designate the heir apparent. Verus, who had little time to enjoy his promotion, promptly died. The frustrated Hadrian then chose Aurelius Antoninus, and as a precaution, just in case he too was planning to die, had him adopt two young men, Verus' son and the young Marcus Aurelius.

After the death of Hadrian the new Imperator, Antoninus Pius, whose very nickname is enough to send the literati scurrying for cover, sold the costly Imperial baubles, reduced taxes, and lived at his own expense on his modest estates as much as possible. These facts alone must have been enough to disgust historians hoping to follow the prying ways of Suetonius and Tacitus. His only real fault was being too much the man of peace; that sort of thing gives opportunists ideas.

The Philosopher Imperator Marcus Aurelius, who succeeded him, had to spend most of his reign dealing with those opportunist ideas and died in a war camp on the Northern frontier. (The Pax Romana wandered off into the mist sometime during this era but, as it folded its tents like the Arabs and silently stole away, it took folks a few years to notice.) Marcus Aurelius saw life clearly and wrote sage advice for everyone. His clear vision unfortunately stopped short of accurately sizing up his son Commodus.

CHAPTER XXV

"Perire omne tempus non studiis datum arbitrabatur."
Pliny *Epistulae*, III, 5

(He thought all time not given to studies was lost.)

While all these stirring events were taking place, some folks were busy writing about them in more-or-less deathless prose and poetry, so a little backward look at the Progress of Literature is in order. The Golden Age of Roman Literature had come to a screeching halt with the death of Augustus in AD 14. All the Golden Age writers who were really on top of things had thoughtfully perished before Augustus (and of natural causes – how amazing!) except for Livy and Ovid, each of whom lingered on about three years after the death of Augustus. Ovid was still in exile out at Tomi, that dismal little one-mule town on the Black Sea, and possibly didn't get the updated news so that he could expire on time. Besides, he was peeved with Augustus, and no doubt hoped a successor would prove more amenable to his pleas for a reprieve. Tiberius was not in the least interested in Ovid's plight. If those leering rumors about Julia and Ovid were true, he might have had his reasons. Probably, though, it was just one more instance of crabbiness on his part. Anyway, Ovid finally gave up the ghost. Livy was probably putting the final touches on those 142 books so that he could toddle off into the sunset as quickly as possible.

By that time the Silver Age writers were already coming on the scene and, having no idea that they were only Second Best, were sharpening their quills with enthusiasm. Seneca the Younger, who divided his time between advising emperors and being exiled or retired, wrote philosophy, satire and nine tragedies guaranteed to give anyone a fit of the dismals. These horrendous plays, which experts say could never have actually been performed, are said to have inspired some of Shakespeare's grislier efforts; Shakespeare managed the hairier deeds largely offstage. (As they require such things as the removal of Lavinia's hands and tongue in *Titus Andronicus*, an onstage performance could have discouraged actors from trying out for the part.)

Seneca's father, sensibly called Seneca the Elder, had also written treatises, but nobody puts him on the preferred list as either Gold or Silver, poor chap. A couple of nice young men named Lucan and Statius wrote epics that nobody nowadays values very much. They might have risen higher in the literary arts if Lucan had not been murdered at a young age by Nero and Statius had not been frightened into writing nauseating praises of Domitian.

Quintilian wrote a grade-A primer for schoolteachers, who according to Martial and the satirists needed some instruction. Although he wrote 37 books of natural history, Pliny the Elder, like Seneca the Elder, missed his chance to be on the Preferred List. He was a tireless scholar who was interested in all about him and who wrote down everything everybody told him. Such a policy is bound to lead to tall tales and scoffers. In AD 79 his inquiring nature led him to sail up under Mount Vesuvius during an eruption to see what was going on. He found out, and they buried him with all honors.

Pliny the Younger, who wisely stayed at home to write an essay while his uncle was investigating Vesuvius, lived to write a great number of letters. In these he not only informed the Imperator about the lamentable financial practices of the Eastern provinces and the weirdness of the Christians, but also acquainted the historian Tacitus with the True Facts concerning Vesuvius' temper tantrum, his uncle's death and his own highly original hunting methods (he sat by a pit, writing letters, and waited for the game to fall in).

There were two great historians of the Silver Age, Tacitus and Suetonius. Neither was enamored of the emperors and both had a gossipy nature, but while Tacitus did occasionally rise to some semblance of impartiality, Suetonius could have been the star reporter for a scandal magazine. Between them they have supplied countless plots to Hollywood.

Petronius, in what is perhaps the first satirical novel, created a rich caricature of Rome's nouveaux riches, a class steadily replacing the old cultured Roman gentry. *The Banquet of Trimalchio* etches on our memory the fabulous wealth, bad Latin and uncouth habits of an ex-slave's son and his shrewish wife. Gellius meanwhile was writing his *Noctes Atticae* or *Nights in Greece*, which isn't nearly as racy as it sounds. He collected bits of literature from former times, on such titillating subjects as geometry and grammar.

CHAPTER XXVI

"Difficile est saturam non scribere."
Juvenal, *Saturae*, I, 30

(It is hard not to write satire.)

Now we must take a deep breath and face up to the poets, who, except for Lucan and Statius already mentioned, were mostly satirists. *Satura* was the one literary form the Romans invented; it started out as a hodgepodge of poetry, prose and anything else the author could think of, and came to be a poetic form that pointed out, usually with a poisoned dart, the difference between what is and what ought to be. Phaedrus did this by means of fables, in which the people he thought needed castigating, or maybe beheading, were usually represented as animals.

Persius the Stoic in his few and brief poems illuminated sharply the decidedly un-Stoic behavior around him. Martial wrote short epigrams impaling various acquaintances. Their names were changed, but evidently that was not enough to prevent their being recognized. After publishing 14 books of his little epigrams, Martial found it best to go and live in Spain. He writes plaintively of his desire for "nights filled with sleep and days free from lawsuits."[23]

The shining light of satire was Juvenal, a brilliant writer and a grouch of the most pronounced description. Pliny the Younger, who was his contemporary, writes to and about many charming and honorable Romans both male and female, but apparently Juvenal never met any of them. Most of his people were foul and despicable, and those who tried to do well always wound up on the short end of the stick. He was the forerunner of the great playwrights of the twentieth century.

Pliny the Younger tells us that many Romans wrote poetry. As a publisher of books had to buy a slave with a strong reading voice and a number of slaves with good penmanship to make hand copies (these truly were manuscripts), getting published in the first century was even harder than getting published in the twenty-first. Therefore, aspiring writers hired halls and read their works aloud, after inviting their long-suffering friends to the readings. Pliny says that those invited did not come, came late, or sneaked out during the reading. These poets must not have been satirists or epigrammists: no one would have dared walk out during one of Martial's readings, for fear he might be the subject of the next epigram. It is sad that these unfortunate writers did not have Nero's advantages; when Nero read or sang his compositions, he had the doors of the hall locked and guards with sharp weapons posted at intervals.

Many literary historians with a passion for neatness say that the Silver Age died along with Marcus Aurelius in AD 180. Some purists insist that it ended with the reign of Hadrian in 138 and that's that. They could be right, since most of the Second Best writers were dead by then. In any case, the Silver Age did not continue after the death of Aurelius.

A Period of Unrest

The next century after the death of Aurelius was, to put it mildly, a period of unrest. It saw continual upheaval and at least 25 emperors, if you count only the ones who lived long enough to be formally recognized. A few folks like Apuleius, who wrote a novel with the interesting subtitle *The Golden Ass* (a title which could have applied to any number of people during this age), continued to write but it was hard, between dodging bodies flying out of the palace windows and changing one's political opinions to fit in with the Emperor of the Day, to produce really great literature. Christian writers such as Tertullian would now produce most notable Latin literature. Tertullian was a Puritan who found plenty of subjects for fiery writing in the behavior of the period. Besides, he was over in Carthage at a considerable distance from the Emperor of the Day.

CHAPTER XXVII

"Sed iam serpentum maior Concordia."
Juvenal, *Saturae*, XIV, 159

(But nowadays there is more harmony among snakes
[than men].)

After the death of Marcus Aurelius, as the second century of our era drew to a close, other aspects of the Roman world besides literature were changing, and not for the better. Commodus, son of Marcus Aurelius, longed to be a gladiator and, if the Fates had not indulged their morbid sense of humor, he would never have been the son of an emperor. After Marcus Aurelius' death on the northern frontier, Commodus hurried back to Rome to enjoy various athletic delights, not all of which were practiced in the amphitheater. While intelligent Imperators like Augustus and Vespasian had shrunk from being hailed as a god and even made jokes about it, the nuttier the rulers were the more they reveled in their supposed deity. Marcus Aurelius may have said that an emperor's purple robe was only sheep hair dyed with the blood of a shellfish,[24] but none of the more unbalanced types believed this; Commodus even surpassed Nero and Caligula in his deity complex. He decided that he was the reincarnation of Hercules (remember the athletic delights) and changed his name to Lucius Aelius Aurelius Commodus Augustus Hercules Romanus Exsuperatorius Amazonius Invictus Felix Pius. He then demanded that the names of the twelve months of the year be changed to match his names.

Commodus was obviously too busy to bother about such trifles as ruling the Empire, and he left governing to his unscrupulous favorites, who treated all citizens – high and low, alike – scandalously. The only good thing these paragons did for the people was to murder Commodus.

Next there was a re-run of the Year of the Four Emperors, which came to a screeching halt with Septimius Severus, a great general, and a fair-to-middling, though grim, emperor. Like so many powerful men, he bred despicable sons and was absolutely determined that they should succeed him. To achieve this lamentable end he pampered the army, which placed his frightful son Caracalla on the throne.

Caracalla began his rule by killing his brother Geta. Then, observing that he was *persona non grata* in Rome and not wanting to show favoritism, he set out with an army on a royal tour of slaughtering people in many lands. The praetorian prefect Macrinus, a man of decision with a first-rate spy system, learned that he was to be one of Caracalla's next victims. Caracalla was soon assassinated and Macrinus – surprise, surprise – was the army's choice for emperor.

Caracalla's mother, who was the only person not applauding his sudden end, produced a niece with a couple of sons who she swore were the children of Caracalla. That she seems to have considered this a recommendation for the little fellows shows the blindness of mother love.

Macrinus evidently misplaced his spy system when he became Imperator and consequently his life was short. One of those new-found "Sons of Caracalla," who rejoiced in the mind-boggling name of Elagabalus, came to Rome from Emesa in Syria to establish the worship of the god whose name he bore. He was made Imperator but he didn't last very long. His gentle brother Alexander set a record for the early third century by staying alive and on the imperial throne for thirteen years.

Alexander's rule was benign but he made the mistake of leaving for the Rhine and, looking back over his shoulder, found the barbarian Maximin was now emperor. Maximin was a good soldier but his misstep was ignoring the civil populace and especially the senate, which had been a nonentity for many years but which suddenly began nominating emperors all over the place and for once had the resolution to stand against Maximin and win in battle. Another dizzying parade of emperors followed and the aging Empire, pausing occasionally in the shadow of an Aurelian or a Probus, continued sliding toward destruction until it came to rest against the wall of Diocletian's determination.

CHAPTER XXVIII

"Maiestate, cui maior e longinquo reverentia."
Tacitus, *Annales*, 47

(Imperial majesty, which inspires greater awe at a distance.)

Diocletian, a commander of the imperial bodyguard, was chosen Imperator by the army after an assortment of murders thinned down the competition and his most likely competitor was finished off by a jealous husband. Until this time Rome had been officially considered a Principate, led by a first citizen who ruled with the consent and the help of the senate. Diocletian turned it into a Dominate, ruled by a master or lord, namely himself.

Diocletian did not follow the hospitable open-door policy of Augustus, Vespasian and Trajan, having observed that what came through the open door in his day was likely to be an assassin. He assumed the god-like status of an Eastern potentate, withdrawing from the people and allowing only favored ones close enough to kiss the hem of his purple robe.

This new potentate was shrewd and it didn't take him long to see that a huge empire with the Mediterranean Sea in its middle could not successfully be managed from a single city over on the west side of things. He therefore divided the Roman Empire into two halves, sensibly called the Eastern Empire and the Western Empire, and made his friend Maximian, who was a great soldier and his loyal follower, his Co-Emperor for the West.

Diocletian set himself up as Jupiter and Maximian as Hercules, which was eerily suitable to the positions they occupied; Diocletian devised new policies and wily plans for carrying them

A Herculean Co-Emperor

out, while Maximian was most at home bashing somebody with a club.

Diocletian had a natural passion for reorganization and he could clearly see that what Rome needed was a first-rate office manager. He enthusiastically set about cleaning out the Imperial filing cabinet, which had gotten crammed with unenforced laws, unfinished business and stray corpses. While setting things in order he enacted a number of measures in which we see the beginning of the European nobility and the feudal system, both of which would make life merry throughout the Middle Ages. During the century of unrest, the governors of the great Roman provinces, especially those farthest from Rome, had ruled as potentates and showed a truly imperial taste for throwing their weight around and raising havoc of all sorts. Diocletian, having split such provinces into several parts, created dukes and counts to oversee the military while the governors carried on civil affairs. He felt that a division of power, and the resulting squabbles sure to arise, should keep all these folk too busy to do major mischief. He was certainly right about the resulting squabbles: dukes and counts collected more or less loyal knights; swords rattled and banners waved. Foundations were being laid for the Age of Chivalry.

The long-lasting chaos, which had given all those governors the illusion that they were absolute rulers, had also ruined the countryside. Battles raging up and down the country and brigands visiting regularly do not have a good effect on productivity. The revenue from lands had fallen, and the various incompetent rulers had responded to the situation by raising taxes. Anybody with a brain could have seen that this was a sure-fire recipe for disaster, but people with brains had not been plentiful in the power structure of the preceding century. Because of the backbreaking load imposed by money-hungry so-called rulers, people had long been burying their portable assets under the giant oak and abandoning lands because of astronomical tax assessments. Diocletian decreed that henceforth people were bound to remain on the land until taxes were paid. If the land was sold, they were sold with it. For these unfortunate folk the old Latin word for "slave," *servus*, was turning into "serf." While the words are not exactly equivalent, neither represented a very desirable form of existence.

To make matters even more cheerful, Diocletian employed hordes of "agents" to see that his many new arrangements were carried out, and no one could move without stepping on a spy.

Having reformed such messy matters as a debased coinage, a rebellious army and obstreperous provinces, Diocletian brought some stability to his world and then appointed two junior colleagues, dutifully called Caesars, to rule subdivisions under himself and Maximian, the Augusti. These Caesars, Galerius in the East under Diocletian and Constantius in the West under Maximian, married the daughters of the Augusti, carried out assigned wars, and generally did what they were told. Diocletian had warned his co-Augustus that a double abdication was in the master plan, and in AD 305, after eleven years of reconditioning the aging machinery of the Roman Empire, he threw in the towel and went off to Split[25] to raise cabbages. This may have been a bit of luck for the cabbage trade, but it was rather hard on the Roman Empire, which promptly relapsed into chaos.

Diocletian should have realized that the eleven years of his reign were not nearly long enough to give everybody time to forget the third-century pastime of making and murdering emperors. The free-for-all broke out again, and when the plaster stopped falling and the corpses were counted, Constantine, the handsome and talented son of Constantius, had defeated Maximian's son Maxentius at the Mulvian Bridge in Rome. He became Co-Emperor with Licinius, who had popped up in one of the ruling factions. This arrangement lasted for some ten years, after which the two emperors quarreled. Constantine settled the quarrel with his usual terminal efficiency and became sole ruler of the Roman Empire.

Constantine wanted to be sole ruler but he liked the idea of dual capitals. He built a second Rome, complete with an artificial seven hills, at Byzantium on the Bosphorus; he also undertook building in Rome itself. There was rebuilding to be done that was not architectural, however, and for that he cast about him for allies. One of these, the Christian Church, would have seemed a very unlikely candidate to a less innovative ruler, but during the long centuries of turmoil it had been growing and progressing. Constantine turned an envious eye to the marvelous organization of bishops and priests that the church contained. Organization had been conspicuously lacking in the Roman Empire for many years, and the Christians seemed to have it in abundance. Perhaps, to an astute leader, this organization would prove useful.

Constantine also had some family connection with Christianity. His father Constantius had been a monotheist and his mother Helena, a Balkan innkeeper's daughter who had been the concubine of Constantius, had excellent reasons for approving of the Christian doctrine that all people are equal.

When Constantine was five years old, Constantius, upon becoming Caesar, had deserted Helena and married Theodora, the daughter of Maximian, by whom he had six children. Helena embraced Christianity ever more thoroughly, and when

Constantine fought his way to imperial power and raised his mother to Imperial dignity, she showed no desire for a messy revenge on the various people she might have been expected to resent; her main interest was the advance of her religion. Observing that the pagans had physical relics on every hand, such as the Very Cave where the wolf nurtured Romulus and Remus on the Palatine and the Very Olive Tree which Athena planted in Athens, Helena went to Jerusalem and brought back various Christian relics, which today adorn Rome's churches. Her forbearing attitude was not shared by her son, who executed various family members, including his eldest son, for mysterious reasons.

Constantine himself claimed that he had won his battle at the Mulvian Bridge under the Banner of the Cross, and he and Licinus in AD 313 issued the Edict of Milan, which gave favored status to the Christians. He hoped that Christianity would be a unifying influence but the longed-for unity kept tripping over the Donatist Christians in North Africa and the Arians in the East.[26] At the Council of Nicaea, in AD 325, a majority vote declared that the Arians were mistaken, but they were not terribly impressed. They continued to divide the Christian world, preaching what they thought was right and consigning all who disagreed with them to a warm future in the infernal regions.

Amazingly, in spite of being constantly called upon to deal with some Christian crisis or other, Constantine found time to complete and improve upon the reforms of Diocletian. Between them they insured the survival of the Roman Empire of the East for another thousand years. The Christian Church, which owed to Constantine its rise from persecuted minority to favored religion, tended to portray him as a saint. Had he actually been a saint, however, both his longevity and his success as an emperor might have been seriously impaired.

It was said that Constantine was for the first ten years of his reign the best of emperors; for the second decade a robber; and for the third a spendthrift.[27] However that may have been, having restored the Roman Empire and uplifted the Christian Church, he was baptized on his deathbed and left the Roman Empire to his three sons, Contantine II, Constantius and Constans. This trio, which was hard enough for a simple Roman citizen to untangle and separate, was rendered still foggier by the varied forms of Christianity they now adopted. By 361 the descendants of Constantine had been eliminated down to Julian the Apostate, who, though reared a Christian, declared himself a devout pagan, elevated pagans to places of honor and went off to war against Persia. He suffered the fate of many other valiant Romans who went off to war against Persia, and the Emperor Sweepstakes began again.

CHAPTER XXIX

"In se magna ruunt: laetis hunc numina rebus posuere."
Lucan, *Pharsalia*, I, 81

(Great things collapse upon themselves; this limit the gods place
on fortune.)

For some years now, during all these stirring events, life had been heating up on the borders of the Empire. The Huns, or Scourges of God as they were sometimes called by the more revenge-minded Christians, had plowed through the Goth territory to the north of the Empire in search of elbow-room, plunder, or just a little Cain-raising. The Goths came clamoring to be admitted to the Roman Empire, which like everybody else they wrongly considered impregnable. Sometimes these barbarians were admitted and sometimes not. In either case they wreaked havoc, sometimes even unintentionally.

The Roman Empire was now forever divided into East and West and the West, due to the fact that the Huns were now sweeping across Europe in that general direction, had the worst of it. In 410 Alaric the Visigoth sacked Rome itself, and the myth of Rome's invulnerability got a nasty blow. The Romans hastily called home their far-flung legions, leaving the Province of Britain, for one, to fend for itself. Neither this nor anything else did much good, and the venerable Empire tottered on toward annihilation.

From time to time a tribe of barbarians roared into Rome and made a terrible mess. Since these stalwart fellows had no written language, they didn't understand about libraries. What was the use of having great rooms stacked full of crackly stuff rolled around a stick? These weird objects burned very easily, however, and the wisdom of the ages went to kindle campfires.

Thanks to the ingenuity of Gaius Sergius Orata, a contemporary of Julius Caesar, Roman houses were often heated by hypocausts, which consisted of hollow floor tiles through which the heat from a basement furnace traveled.[28] The barbarians, tromping across the floors in their bare feet, broke all records for the standing high jump when they stepped on the hot tiles. After loudly intoning many a wild North Country oath, they usually knocked the offending tiles and most of the rest of the paving out of the floor. Since incidents like these were increasingly frequent, barbarian raids seldom added much to the comfort and beauty of Rome.

In 476, after a sickening series of weak Emperors of the West, German soldiers in the Roman army decided that they had played Charades long enough and proclaimed their leader Odoacer king of Italy. He patted the last emperor, young Romulus Augustulus, on the head and sent him out to play. Then, politely calling in the senate to ask for the ancient powers conferred on an Imperator, through it he offered the whole shebang to Zeno the Eastern Emperor provided that Zeno would appoint Odoacer ruler of the West. Zeno granted what he had no power to refuse and the Western Roman Empire toddled off into the sunset.

Of course people went on calling themselves Romans for hundreds of years, and for a thousand years the Roman Emperor of the East, complete with toga and senate, ruled in Constantinople. The Emperors of the East said that this was a clear triumph for their Christianity. Be that as it may, their Christian capital of Constantinople was ravaged in 1204 when the Crusaders, having come to the Near East to defend Christianity from strange religions, evidently failed to recognize fellow Christians when they saw them and rampaged through Constantinople. She never recovered from this tragedy and finally fell to the Muslim Turks in 1453.

For many centuries Rome had been as much an idea as a reality, and even as Constantinople fell, the Renaissance, or "Rebirth of the Classical World," was beginning in Italy. The Eternal City would carry into succeeding ages her dual personality of an Earthy City and a battered Bird of Paradise that, even with her tail feathers sadly bedraggled, would continue to rise and inspire humankind.

Urbs Aeterna

REALITY CHECK

Except for a few quotes from standard reference works and noted historians, the information in this book comes from Vergil, Livy, and other Roman writers. The early stories cannot be taken as absolute factual history, as even Livy often gives two versions of the same story, neither verifiable. These are valuable because they represent Roman history as the Romans themselves accepted and revered it. Even as they revered their ancestors, however, the Romans had a remarkable quality of calling a spade a spade. They had no compunction about telling all when the Roman army broke and ran, as they did at the river Allia. Roman insights into human nature and their recording of facts ironic as well as heroic have made this book possible. Everything written here is the result, not of the author's invention, but of her selection of and approach to Latin literature.

NOTES

1. Romulus and Remus: Livy, *Ab Urbe Condita*, I, 5–6
2. Venus the Bald: Servius, *Ad Aenean*, I, 720
3. The small round temple of Venus Cloacina, which stands in the Roman Forum near the Senate House, is very ancient. It is generally thought to have been built in gratitude for the Cloaca Maxima, which was Rome's first sewer and possibly the first in the Western world. To understand the Romans' thankfulness one has only to imagine a hot day in a large city which had no sewer.
4. Hannibal: Juvenal, *Saturae*, X, 153. Juvenal is alluding to the process of heating rocks and then pouring vinegar on them to split them in order to gain a foothold. While this method works, it is hardly practical on a large scale for a moving army.
5. Spanish Bride: Livy, *Ab Urbe Condita*, 26. 50
6. Cato and the Women: Livy, *Ab Urbe Condita*, 34
7. Boys excluded from Senate: Gellius, *Noctes Atticae*, I, 23
8. Marius' Escape: Plutarch, *Marius*
9. Cicero and the Gauls: The Allobroges, a Gallic tribe, had sent envoys to Rome to discuss bad conditions in their province. The Catilinarian conspirators approached these envoys and offered money and aid if they would join the conspiracy and help overthrow the Roman government. The Gauls consulted their Roman patron, Quintus Fabius Sanga, about this proposition. He took the whole story to Cicero, who instructed the

Gauls to pretend to join the conspiracy, get the whole thing in writing, and arrange with him a convenient time and place to be caught with the papers. They were rewarded and the conspirators who supplied the evidence were jailed.

10. Caesar's Reforms , "Caesar, Gaius Julius," *Oxford Classical Dictionary*

11. Cato in Jail: Gellius, *Noctes Atticae*, IV, 10

12. Bratuspantium: City in Gaul belonging to the Bellovaci. When Caesar approached it with his army, it sent envoys out to him to surrender. *De Bello Gallico*, II, 13

13. Octavian's luck: Shakespeare, *Antony and Cleopatra*, Act II, Scene 3

14. Julia's suitors: Suetonius, *Divus Augustus*, 73, 1

15. Theater: Cicero, *Ad Familiares*, 7.1

16. Panthers: Cicero, *Ad Familiares*, 2.11

17. Clodia: Cicero, *Pro Caelio*

18. Glass: Isidore of Seville, *Etymologiae sive Origines*

19. Temple: Ehrenberg & Jones, *Documents illustrating the reigns of Augustus and Tiberius, 102* (Oxford, 1955)

20. Vespasian's Economy: Suetonius, *Vespasian*, 18

21. Sun Laws: Butti & Perlin, *A Golden Thread*, 19, 27

22. Sabina: *Scriptores Historiae Augustae: Hadrian*

23. Lawsuits: Martial, *Epigrams*, II, 90

24. Shellfish: Marcus Aurelius, *Meditations*

25. Split: ancient Spalato, a city on the eastern coast of the Adriatic Sea

26. Arian: A Christian who believed with Arius of Alexandria that Jesus was not quite divine, although superhuman
Donatist: A follower of Donatus, an uncomfortably Puritanical Christian bishop in North Africa who believed the value of Christian sacraments and the safety of Christian souls depended on the holiness of the cleric, and that anyone who had ever faltered in the face of possible martyrdom had no business in the Christian Church. While this may have been an admirable sentiment, it was hardly likely to increase membership.

27. Constantine's Changes: This intriguing statement is made by Household in *Rome Republic and Empire*. The statement may

stem from the habit Constantine developed of wresting city taxes from municipal governments and later spending them upon the magnificent Eastern potentate palaces and garments he acquired for himself. Household also mentions in passing various family members Constantine murdered. One can see why he waited to be baptized until he was on his deathbed; earlier conformity to the known preferences of Christian spokesmen might have seriously interrupted his lifestyle and his governing techniques.

28. De Camp explains in *The Ancient Engineers* that Orata started with heated tanks for growing seafood in the winter and branched out.

GLOSSARY

Ab Urbe Condita (AUC): "From the founding of the city," April 21, 753 BC.

Aedile: an elected official in Rome whose responsibilities came to include the circus games.

Alba Longa: ancient town in Italy near Rome.

Alexander the Great: King of Macedon 336–323 BC. Conquered Greece, Asia Minor, Persia, Palestine, Egypt and parts of India.

Alexander, Marcus Aurelius Severus: Roman Emperor 222–35.

Aurelian: Roman Emperor 270–75. He defeated many enemies of Rome, restored a measure of stability, and built the Aurelian wall around the city, which could no longer be considered safe from attack.

Bosphorus: strait between Thrace and Asia Minor.

Brundisium: a port city in Southeast Italy from which people usually embark for Greece.

Censor: One of two Roman magistrates elected every five years to take the census and censor morals. Their term of office was 18 months.

Cynic: a follower of Diogenes of Greece, who believed in simplicity and honesty. He went about with a lantern, peering into people's faces and saying he was looking for an honest man. Failing to find anyone who met his standards, he went and lived in a barrel.

Denarius: a Roman coin worth about $1, or $2, or some other amount, according to the good or lousy state of a given economy.

Emesa: City in Syria famed for the worship of Baal.

Hades: the underworld where the ancients believed that everyone went after death.

Harpies: monsters with the heads of maidens and the bodies of birds.

Heliocaminus: literally, a "solar furnace;" a sun-room. In Rome and environs such a room would have southwest openings covered with glass or mica and would get very warm.

Imperator: Roman title for a commanding general in the army; it became a title of honor for a commander who had won a victory and afterwards the title emperor.

Manuscript: that which is written by hand.

Ovid: Publius Ovidius Naso, 43 BC–AD 17. Author of *Ars Amatoria*, *Amores*, *Metamorphoses*, *Fasti*.

Pomerium: space kept free of buildings inside and outside a city wall.

Praetor: elected Roman judicial magistrate.

Propraetor: magistrate who had extended governorship.

Praetorian Prefect: commander of the Praetorian Guard, which became the bodyguard troop of the emperor.

Princeps: first Citizen or Chief, the title that Augustus assumed when he became ruler.

Probus: Roman emperor 276–82. He continued the work of Aurelian and dealt with the growing barbarian threat from the north.

Sibyl: a prophetess and priestess of Apollo; the best-known one lived at Cumae on the Bay of Naples.

Skeptic: a person who believes that everyone's knowledge, including his own, is severely limited if not totally absent. Protogoras and the Greek Sophists popularized this view, which was taken perhaps to extremes by the French philosopher Descartes, who said he doubted the existence of all things except himself; he knew that he existed because something had to be doing all the doubting.

Sparta: capital city of Laconia, in Greece.

Stoic: a follower of the beliefs of Zeno the Greek, who believed in putting aside all passions and indulgences and living for duty. This philosophy led to great achievements by those with the moxie to follow it, but it made little headway with the vast majority of the human race.

Strait of the Dardanelles: narrow water passage between Asia Minor and Europe.

Ulysses (Odysseus): Greek king of the island of Ithaca who was a leader in the Trojan War.

Vitruvius: Roman engineer employed by Julius Caesar; he wrote *De Architectura*, which became the bible of builders for 15 centuries.

MAJOR POINTS IN ROMAN HISTORY

753–509 BC (0–244 AUC): Kingdom

753–509 BC: Seven Kings of Rome: Romulus, Numa Pompilius, Tullus Hostilius, Ancus Marcius, Tarquinius Priscus, Servius Tullius and Tarquinius Superbus.

509–27 BC: Republic

509–265 BC: Early Republic
509 Annually elected magistrates
451–450 Law of Twelve Tables written
390 Rome sacked by the Gauls
367 Consulship opened to plebeians
312 Censorship of Appius Claudius Caecus
298–290 Third Samnite War
281–272 War with King Pyrrhus
279 Pyrrhic victory

265–133 BC: Middle Republic
264–241 First Punic War
218–201 Second Punic War
196 Flamininus proclaims freedom for Greece
184 Censorship of Cato
149–146 Third Punic War

133–27 BC: Late Republic
133 Murder of Tiberius Gracchus
112–106 War with Jugurtha in Numidia
107–100 Repeated consulships of Gaius Marius
82–79 Sulla Dictator
73–71 Revolt of Spartacus the Gladiator
63 Consulship of Cicero
60 First Triumvirate of Julius Caesar, Pompeyu the Great and Crassus
59 Consulship of Caesar
58–50 Caesar's Gallic campaign
49–46 Civil War between Caesar and the senatorial forces
46 Suicide of Cato Uticensis
44 Assassination of Caesar
43 Second Triumvirate of Mark Antony, Octavian and Lepidus
42 Battle of Philippi
39 Marriage of Octavian and Livia
31 Battle of Actium
27 Octavian given title of Augustus

27 BC–AD 476: Empire

27 BC–AD 284: Principate
27 BC–AD 14 Augustus Imperator
23 BC Death of Marcellus
12 bc Marriage of Tiberius and Julia
9 bc Death of Drusus, Augustus' eldest stepson
ad 4 Adoption of Tiberius by Augustus
14–37 Tiberius Imperator
19 Death of Germanicus
37–41 Caligula Imperator
41–54 Claudius Imperator
43 Conquest of Britian
54–68 Nero Imperator
54–9 Nero's "good years," guided by Seneca
67 Vespasian's Judean campaign
68–9 Year of the Four Emperors

69–79 Vespasian Imperator
70 Capture of Jerusalem by Titus, son of Vespasian
79–81 Titus Imperator
80 Completion of the Collosseum, or Flavian Amphitheater
81–96 Domitian Imperator
96–8 Nerva Imperator
98–117 Trajan Imperator
117–38 Hadrian Imperator
138–61 Antoninus Pius Imperator
161–80 Marcus Aurelius Imperator
180–192 Commodus Imperator
193–211 Septimius Severus Emperor
211–84 Military unrest and political disorder; many emperors

AD 284–476: Dominate
284–305 Diocletian emperor
293 Division of empire into Eastern and Western; four rulers
305 Abdication of Diocletian and Maximian
306–37 Constantine emperor
313 Edict of Milan, confirming religious toleration for Christians
324 Founding of Constantinople
325 Council of Nicaea
337–476 Varied emperors of varied abilities
410 Visigoths sack Rome
455 Vandals sack Rome
476 Romulus Augustulus deposed by Odoacer

BIBLIOGRAPHY

Balsdon, J.P.V.D. 1998. *Roman Women*. New York: Barnes and Noble Books.

Butti, K. & Perlin, J. 1980. *A Golden Thread*. New York: Litton Educational Publishing.

Creighton, Mandell. 2000. *Primer History of Rome*. London: Wimbledon Publishing Company.

De Camp, L.S. 1963. *The Ancient Engineers*. New York: Ballantyne Books.

Duff, J.W. 1962. *A Literary History of Rome: Golden Age*. London: Ernest Benn Ltd.

Duff, J.W. 1968. *A Literary History of Rome: Silver Age*. London: Ernest Benn Ltd.

Durant, W. 1944. *Caesar and Christ*. New York: Mahony & Roese.

Grant, M. 1976. *The Fall of the Roman Empire: A Reappraisal*. London: Nelson & Sons.

Grimshaw, W. 1851. *Roman History*. Philadelphia: Lippincott, Grambo & Company.

Household, H.W. 1936. *Rome Republic and Empire*. London: J.M. Dent & Sons, Ltd.

Leighton, R.F. 1881. *A History of Rome*. New York: Clark & Maynard.

Lewis, Naphtali & Reinhold, Meyer. 1966. *Roman Civilization*. New York: Harper & Row.

INDEX

This index covers the text, notes, glossary and chronology. References to illustrations are given in italics. Entries for references found in the notes have the suffix 'n', those in the glossary have 'g', and those in the chronology have 'c'. References to persons with multiple names are given in the form in which they appear predominantly in the text, for example 'Caesar, Julius' rather than 'Julius Caesar'. Entries are in word-by- word order, where a space precedes a letter, for example, 'Helen of Troy' precedes 'Helena'.

Vergil for Beginners
A Dual Approach to Early Vergil Study
Rose Williams

This ancillary text for first-year high school Latin students or for students beginning their second semester of college Latin presents six short selections from Vergil's *Aeneid*, each accompanied by grammar exercises and vocabulary aids.

The design of the book works for either grammar-based or reading-based approaches, or some mixture of the two. The different sections in the book can be used in whatever order the teacher finds most effective. Grammar exercises present and review key elements of grammar for each reading selection, and Latin synonyms promote reading comprehension. The use of this reading supplement near the end of students' most basic Latin study will help them develop the ability to handle Latin literature as they reach an advanced level.

Student Text: xii + 96 pp. (2006) 6" x 9" Paperback
ISBN 978-0-86516-628-8
Teacher's Manual: (2007) 6" x 9" Paperback
ISBN 978-0-86516-629-5

Cicero the Patriot
Rose Williams

Lighthearted in tone but faithful to the facts, this readable volume interweaves the story of Cicero's private life and feelings with the development of his public life and his literary output. Details and commentary on Cicero's speeches, letters, and philosophical writings highlight the events in his world that served as background for some of the most poignant, as well as the most dramatic, writing ever done in Latin. Williams shows the human side of the renowned orator and thereby allows the reader to savor Cicero's dreams, disappointments, and pursuits.

Students will enjoy this volume that completes the gaps in their knowledge of Cicero. The ethical principles that propelled the orator to courageous and ultimately fatal undertakings are told with memorable twists of language that offer comic relief and enhance appreciation for Cicero as a total person.

An extensive glossary explaining customs and practices such as *salutationes* and the Lupercalia along with a timeline of Cicero's major works and the events of his life make this book an invaluable resource for both students and teachers.

Student Text: vi + 92 pp. (2004) 6" x 9" Paperback
ISBN 978-0-86516-587-8
Teacher's Manual: xi + 74 pp. (2004) 6" x 9" Paperback
ISBN 978-0-86516-588-5

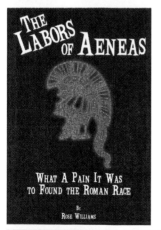

Labors of Aeneas
What a Pain It Was to Found the Roman Race
Rose Williams

This paperback book retells the story of the *Aeneid* in a lighthearted and understandable manner with humorous insights and asides. This volume makes Books I–XII of Vergil's *Aeneid* enjoyable and easy to follow and may be used in conjunction with the Latin text of Vergil's *Aeneid* in high school classrooms.

vi + 108 pp. (2003) 6" x 9" Paperback, ISBN 978-0-86516-556-4

BOLCHAZY-CARDUCCI PUBLISHERS, INC.
WWW.BOLCHAZY.COM

The Young Romans

Rose Williams

    This beginning Latin reader, designed for the younger student, tells in simple Latin the stories of Roman children who played a significant role in Roman history. Ascanius, Camilla, Cloelia, Alexander the boy emperor, and many more are highlighted in twenty chapters that include pictures, crossword puzzles, special activities, English words from Latin, and simple thought questions.

Student Text: vii + 128 pp. (2003) 6" x 9" Paperback
ISBN 978-0-86516-670-7
Teacher's Manual: v + 176 pp. (2004) 6" x 9" Paperback
ISBN 1-8343310-81-3

Duces Romanorum
Roman Profiles in Courage

Rose Williams

    This graded reader, designed for the intermediate-level student, tells in chronological order stories of the people who forged the Roman world from the city's founding through the emperors. Stories of Aeneas, Scaevola, Germanicus, and more are included, all with an introduction to their historical context, vocabulary, content questions, and a pertinent motto. The subjunctive mood and other advanced grammar as well as direct quotes from Roman authors help the student prepare for reading authentic texts. A complete vocabulary appears at the end.

Student Text: vii + 125 pp. (2002) 6" x 9" Paperback
ISBN 1-898855-47-1
Teacher's Manual: ix + 166 pp. (2002) 6" x 9" Paperback
ISBN 1-898855-49-8

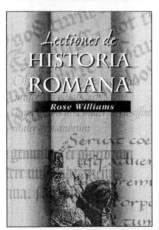

Lectiones de Historia Romana

Rose Williams

    These short chronological readings on events that shaped the Roman world (birth and growth of Rome, wars, age of emperors, decline of empire) are designed for all students of Latin, from entry level on. Grammar and vocabulary gradually increase in the lessons, which contain vocabulary notes, a pertinent motto, and easy questions in Latin. The last third of the book contains no new grammar, to build student confidence. A complete vocabulary appears at the end.

Student Text: 102 pp. (2001) 6" x 9" Paperback
ISBN 1-898855-41-2
Teacher's Manual: 76 pp. (2001) 6" x 9" Paperback
ISBN 1-898855-45-5

BOLCHAZY-CARDUCCI PUBLISHERS, INC.
WWW.BOLCHAZY.COM